Plays
for the
Holidays

Historical and Cultural Celebrations

Anne Siebert
Raymond C. Clark

Illustrations by **Marc Nadel**

PRO LINGUA ◉ ASSOCIATES

Pro Lingua Associates, Publishers
P.O. Box 1348
Brattleboro, Vermont 05302 USA
Office: 802 257 7779
Orders: 800 366 4775
Email: info@ProLinguaAssociates.com
WebStore www.ProLinguaAssociates.com
SAN: 216-0579

At Pro Lingua
our objective is to foster an approach
to learning and teaching that we call
interplay, *the* **inter***action of language*
learners and teachers with their materials,
with the language and culture,
and with each other in active, creative
and productive **play.**

Plays for the Holidays was designed by Arthur A. Burrows. It was set in Adobe Times, a digital font based on Times New Roman, at present one of the most popular type faces. Being consistent in weight and color, with sharp neoclassical serifs, it is easy to read even when set small or printed badly. Its bold is bold and italic legible. Times New Roman is an early Twentieth Century type developed either by Victor Lardent in London in 1931 or by Starling Burgess in the United States in 1904 – there is historical controversy. No matter who drew the original Times New Roman, it was drawn from classical Roman fonts initially popular in the 1700's because they adapted well for setting Greek. The same characteristics have made it the most common modern type for phonetic alphabets and multilingual texts. The display type on the cover/title page and the unit titles is Palatino. Many display types were used for the play titles.

This book was printed and bound by Sheridan Books, Ann Arbor, Michigan.

Printed in the United States of America
Second, revised printing 2014. 2450 copies in print.

Contents

Student's Guide

You can use this book to learn about and enjoy the holidays in America. For each holiday there is a play about the holiday. The book begins with Labor Day so you can begin in September and follow the holidays through the school year. This is how you can use the book to understand and enjoy the holidays and improve your English:

Page 1   *Look* at the **picture of a typical holiday celebration** and *read* the information under it. *Talk* about the picture and the information. Share what you know about the holiday.

Page 2   **Prepare for the Play:** *Listen* **and** *Write.*
Your teacher or another student will read the short dictation in the back of the book. Listen and write it down. This dictation introduces the reading about the play.

Background Reading for the Play.
Read this passage. It gives information about the play.
The reading will help you understand and perform the play.

Page 3   **Answer.**
After you do the reading, *fill in the blanks* in these sentences. First try to do it without looking at the reading. Then go back to the reading to check your answers.

Pronounce. You will use these words in the play. It is important to *say* them well.
One syllable (part of the word) is louder than the others. This is called stress.
It is important in speaking English. After the words you will see some phrases that are in the play. It is important to say these phrases smoothly and quickly. *Practice* saying them.

Page 4   *Match.*
Put the parts of the sentence together. This helps you *understand the meanings* of the word.

Write and Say.
Write all the sentences from the match. Then practice *saying* them quickly and naturally.

Page 5   **Talk About the Poster.**
The picture is an ad or **poster for the play**. Think and talk about it before you perform the play.

Page 6   **The Playbill.**
Decide who will be the different people in the play. You can *write* their names right on the Playbill. You can copy this page and give it to the audience if you perform the play.

Page 7   **The Play.**
First, *read* the play slowly and carefully. *Ask* questions as you read. It is important to *understand* the words and the lines in the play. Then *practice* the play until you can do it easily. Then, you can *do* it with props (clothes and things) and sounds. Finally, you can *read or perform* the play for an audience, or tape it and watch it yourselves.

After reading the play, ask questions and discuss the American history and culture in the play. Why do Americans celebrate this history with a holiday?

Labor Day

The first Monday in September is Labor Day. It became a national holiday in 1894. It is a three-day weekend. For many people it is the end of summer. Many families spend this last summer weekend at the beach, the lakes, or the mountains. Then it is back to work. Vacations are over. Students go back to school. Fall is coming.

Prepare for the play. Listen and write.

In the 1800s, _____

_____

_____

_____

_____

_____

_____

Background Reading for the Play

Peter McGuire was a poor immigrant. His family and thousands of others emigrated from Ireland in the mid 1800s. They wanted to escape the terrible conditions in their countries and make a better life for themselves.

However, New York City was a crowded, dirty place. Immigrants lived in tenements with six to eight people crowded into small rooms. There was little money. Everybody had to work ten to twelve hours a day, children too.

Peter hated that. He wanted to change things. He went to night school, studied economics, and met with others to see what they could do. They decided to unite the workers into a worker's union.

They marched and protested and went on strike. Often they were beaten up by the police. Slowly as a result of strikes, the workers began to win. They got an eight-hour working day and job security. For this, Peter McGuire is known as the father of Labor Day.

Answer

1. Peter McGuire was from _____.

2. His _____ wanted to escape from the terrible conditions in _____.

3. In _____ _____ _____, they lived in tenements.

4. Everybody worked _____ to _____ hours a _____.

5. Peter went to _____ school.

6. Peter helped the workers form a _____.

7. The workers went on _____.

8. Peter is known as the _____ of Labor Day.

— /
Pronounce

/ — —	/ — —	/ — —	— / —
organize	immigrant	tenement	condition
unionize	carpenter	factory	important
celebrate	tool maker	company	apprentice
recognize	dock worker	brotherhood	
		holiday	

a terrible situation	a few dollars	a better life
a good speaker	a Labor Day parade	a big day
a huge success	a few years	a national holiday
a special day	a special event	an eight-hour day

Match

1. _____ To organize   A. is a person who works with wood.

2. _____ To unionize   B. is to see, listen to, and respect.

3. _____ To celebrate   C. is a person who is learning a trade.

4. _____ To recognize   D. is to put things in order.

5. _____ An immigrant   E. is to form unions.

6. _____ A carpenter   F. is a person who loads and unloads boats.

7. _____ A tool maker   G. is a person who moves into a new country.

8. _____ A dock worker   H. is a person who makes tools.

9. _____ An apprentice   I. is to honor and enjoy a person or event.

Copy and say

1. *To organize* _____

2. _____

3. _____

4. _____

5. _____

6. _____

7. _____

8. _____

9. _____

TODAY!

For Labor Day

At the ESL Playhouse

Workers Unite!

The Story of Peter McGuire, the Father of Labor Day

Peter McGuire fights for justice.
The workers must march!

Talk about the poster.

The ESL Playhouse

PRESENTS

Workers Unite!

The Story of Peter McGuire
Father of Labor Day

PRODUCED BY _____

DIRECTED BY _____

THE CAST

Narrator _____

Peter McGuire's Father _____

Peter McGuire _____

Peter McGuire's Mother _____

Peter's Friend _____

Peter's Manager _____

Chorus _____

_____

_____

_____

TIME: 1863

PLACE: The play opens in a New York City tenement house

STORY: A young Irish immigrant makes life better for all workers.

Workers Unite!

Narrator: The year is 1863. America is at war. It is a war between the States, the North and the South. It is the Civil War. The McGuire family does not have enough money to pay the rent and buy food.

Father McGuire: I'll enlist in the army. It will provide at least a few dollars for the family. We have nothing. No work, no money, and six children to feed. It's a terrible situation.

Peter McGuire: Don't worry, Father. I'll take care of the family. I'm only eleven, but I can shine shoes and clean stores. I'll help to support Mother and our family. I can even work in a factory. Don't worry, Father.

Chorus: Thousands of immigrants
Came to America
Looking for work,
For a new life,
A better life
For themselves,
For their children!

Narrator: At first, they did not find a better life. Immigrant men, women, and even children had to work very hard. They often worked ten to twelve hours a day in factories under terrible conditions.

Mother McGuire: I am so tired and so sick. I should stay home today, but if I don't go, I'll lose my job. Somebody else will take it. I have to go or I'll have no job. *(sighs and cries)*

Chorus: Go to work!
Go to work!
Sick or not
You must always
Go to work!
That's the law!
That's the law!

Peter: Someday this will change. This must change. Someday, there will be new laws. Someday! But how? When?

Narrator: When Peter was seventeen, he became an apprentice in a piano shop.

Peter: This is better than shining shoes and the pay is better, but the hours are long. There is more to life than work, work, work. Don't we workers have any rights?

Chorus: Peter, Peter!
Go to school!
Go to night school!
Study and learn
The problems of the day,
The problems of the day,
Study and learn!
Study and learn!

Narrator: And that's what he did. Peter studied economics. He learned. He talked to others about their terrible working conditions. They talked about starting a union. He learned that to make change you have to organize. You have to get people together. You have to unionize.

Mother: Where are you going, Peter? It's late.

Peter: I'm going to another meeting, Mother. We're going to organize. The factory owners can't push us around anymore. We need shorter working hours. And we have rights, too! We're going to start a union!

Mother: Oh, Peter! You will get into trouble! You'll be hurt, or killed! Peter, I'm worried about you. They say you're a trouble maker. They say you're disturbing the peace. Peter, please be careful! Be careful!

Peter: Don't worry, Mother. I can take care of myself! But this is important. We workers must stand up for our rights. We can't work long, long hours for nothing!

Chorus: They organized.
They marched in the streets
One-hundred thousand
Marched in the streets
An eight-hour day!
An eight-hour day!
This is what we want,
An eight-hour day!

Narrator: Sometimes Peter and his fellow marchers were beaten by the police. Later, Peter's boss called him into the office.

Peter's Manager: I'm sorry, Peter, but you no longer have a job with us. You're a trouble maker. You don't belong with our company.

Peter: Then, I'll find a job somewhere else.

Manager: Sure, good luck, but nobody will hire you. You only cause problems — you and your union.

Narrator: And nobody would hire him. They thought he was a trouble maker and didn't want him around.

Peter's friend: Peter, you're a good speaker. People listen to you. They believe you. Why don't you travel and make speeches. Talk to the different trades like the carpenters, the tool makers, and the dock workers. Tell them to unionize and demand better conditions.

Peter: That's exactly what I'll do. That is what needs to be done!

Narrator: He went up and down the East Coast, and he went west to St. Louis. He went to Chicago, talking and urging workers to demand better conditions.

Peter: Gentlemen, trade workers. We are the workers who are building this country! We are making America rich with our work and skills. Where's our reward?

Chorus: Increase our wages!
Increase our wages!
This is what we want!
Increase our wages!

Narrator: The workers listened. They organized. Peter's words inspired them. They cheered him! They believed him! They made him Secretary of the Brotherhood of Carpenters and Joiners of America.

Peter: Now is the time to show America that we workers are important, strong, and united. We need to show America that we are proud of what we do. Let's have a Labor Day parade!

Narrator: So, on September 5, 1882, the first Labor Day parade was held in New York City. It was a big day. Twenty-thousand workers marched on Broadway. They had picnics and fireworks, too.

Chorus: Eight hours for work!
Eight hours for rest!
Eight hours for recreation!
Eight hours for work!
Eight hours for rest!
And recreation, too!

Narrator: The parade was a huge success. The next year there was another. Within a few years, other cities began to celebrate Labor Day, and in 1894 Labor Day was made into a national holiday.

Peter's friend: Peter, did you hear the good news? Congress voted Labor Day to be a national holiday! Isn't that something!

Peter McGuire: Wonderful! Now, we have a special day for all of us, not for one person or a special event, but a day for all working people.

Narrator: And slowly things changed. In many industries, the management began to recognize the workers. And an eight-hour day became standard. Workers were not afraid for their jobs. Life became easier and better.

Peter: I do believe that in America all things are possible. Yes, all things are possible.

Narrator: Peter McGuire died in 1906 at the age of 54. He spent most of his life making things better for the American worker. Today, he is known as the father of Labor Day.

Chorus: We celebrate Labor Day!
With picnics, speeches,
And big parades!
The end of summer,
The beginning of fall!
Let's celebrate it,
One and all!

Columbus Day

The Columbus Day holiday is now celebrated on the second Monday in October. It marks the discovery of the New World by Christopher Columbus. Actually, Columbus landed on an island in the Bahamas on October 12, 1492. Today some large cities celebrate with parades and other activities in honor of this explorer.

Prepare for the play. Listen and write.

Until 1492, _____

_____

_____

_____

_____

_____

_____

Background Reading for the Play

In the 1400s, the people of Europe wanted the silks, spices, and gold that travelers like Marco Polo were bringing from the East — from China, Japan, and India. These lands were called the Indies. But travel over land was long and dangerous. Was there another way to the Indies?

Christopher Columbus was born in Genoa, Italy in 1451. He loved ships, and he loved the sea, and he thought there was another way to reach the Indies. He believed that a person could sail west from Spain and reach the Indies. He convinced Queen Isabella of Spain that he would make Spain rich if she would give the ships for the journey.

On August 3, 1492, with three ships and a crew of 90 men, he began the long, difficult journey. They did not see land for over two months. The crew wanted to turn back, but finally on October 12, 1492 they found land. It was a small island in the Bahamas. He was sure it was the Indies.

The native people welcomed him. He called them Indians, but they were really the Taino tribe, a friendly, gentle people. Columbus forced them to look for gold.

Seven months later, Columbus returned to Spain. He brought back samples of gold, native birds, and even native people that he had captured. He made three more trips to the New World before he died in 1506.

Answer

1. Columbus was born in _____.

2. He believed you could sail _____ and reach the Indies.

3. Queen Isabella gave him _____ships.

4. They did not see land for over two _____.

5. Finally they reached a small _____ in the Bahamas.

6. Columbus was sure he had reached the _____.

7. The native people _____him.

8. Columbus made _____ trips to the New World.

— /

Pronounce

/ -	/ - -	- / -	- / -
painter	dangerous	expensive	discouraged
servant	majesty	advisor	Bahamas
journey	difficult	persisted	October
surgeon	wonderful	rewarded	
	beautiful		

from the East	of his travels	along the way	to the Indies
of the world	to the people	for the journey	in the sea
in the Bahamas	for the queen	to other islands	

Match

1. _____ An advisor		A. is the opposite of ugly.
2. _____ A surgeon		B. made a dangerous journey.
3. _____ A painter		C. is to give a prize for good work.
4. _____ A servant		D. gives advice.
5. _____ A journey		E. loses hope.
6. _____ Difficult		F. is a medical doctor.
7. _____ Beautiful		G. is the opposite of easy.
8. _____ Expensive		H. is an artist.
9. _____ To persist		I. is a long trip.
10. _____ To reward		J. is a person who works for another.
11. _____ A discouraged person		K. is to keep doing something without stopping.
12. _____ Columbus		L. is the opposite of cheap.

Copy and say

1. An advisor _____

2. _____

3. _____

4. _____

5. _____

6. _____

7. _____

8. _____

9. _____

10. _____

11. _____

12. _____

Now at the ESL Playhouse
OUR NEXT ATTRACTION

Land Ho!

Christopher Columbus Discovers an Unknown World

Across the great ocean they sailed.
Fear and danger
And, at last, the great discovery!

Talk about the poster.

The ESL Playhouse

PRESENTS

Land Ho!

Christopher Columbus
Makes a Dangerous Journey

PRODUCED BY _____

DIRECTED BY _____

THE CAST

Narrator _____

Christopher Columbus _____

Queen Isabella of Spain _____

Sailor 1 _____

Sailor 2 _____

Indian 1 _____

Indian 2 _____

Chorus _____

_____

_____

_____

TIME: 1492

PLACE: Spain and the New World

STORY: Columbus goes on a dangerous journey for Spain.

Your Playbill

Land Ho!

Narrator: In 1492, Spain and most of Europe wanted gold, silk, and spices from the East — China, Japan, and India. These lands were called the Indies.

Chorus: Gold and silk and spices,
Gold and silk and spices!
We want them all!
Gold and silk and spices!

Narrator: They had heard of Marco Polo. He had told of his travels, and had brought back such things. But he had traveled over land, a long and dangerous journey. There were bandits along the way. They needed a faster, safer route. But where? How?

Columbus: I know how to get to the Indies. We can go by sea. The earth is round and we can get there by sailing west. I can go across the great ocean.

Narrator: So, he went to Queen Isabella of Spain.

Columbus: Dear Queen, Your Majesty, I need three ships and a good crew. I shall sail to the Indies, and I'll bring back the riches of the world. Dear Queen, can you help me?

Queen Isabella: No, Columbus. It's too expensive, too dangerous. My advisors tell me it's not possible to do what you want. They say you are a madman.

Narrator: But Columbus persisted. He was a man who never gave up. He asked again. The answer was no. But after he asked Queen Isabella a third time, she finally said yes.

Queen Isabella: Yes, Columbus, go! Bring back the riches for Spain. But remember, you must also bring Christianity to the people of the Indies. Where Spain goes, Christianity goes too.

Columbus: Yes, dear Queen, all we meet will become Christian. And we shall bring back gold and silver, spices and silk. Spain shall be the envy of Europe.

Queen Isabella: Go, Columbus, go! Your three ships await you!

Chorus: The Nina, The Pinta,
The Santa Maria.
The Nina, The Pinta,
The Santa Maria.
Three ships in all,
Ready to sail
The unknown sea!
Ready to sail
The unknown sea!

Columbus: Men, we are ready for the journey. Say your prayers and your good-byes. It will be a long, difficult journey. But, take heart, men. Great riches await us.

Sailor 1: What do you think? Will we ever see our families again? Perhaps we will never return home!

Sailor 2: I hear there are monsters in the sea! Let us pray for good weather and good fortune. May God protect us!

Columbus: Men, let us be on our way. The weather is good. Let us sail today!

Chorus: Ninety men got in their ships,
Sailors and servants
And a surgeon, too.
Carpenters, painters
Made up the crew
That sailed from Spain,
From Palos, Spain.
On the third of August in ninety-two!

Columbus: Men, the first man who sees land will be rewarded. He will receive my silk jacket and a prize from the Queen. Keep your eyes open, men. Keep them open!

Narrator: But after weeks and weeks, there was no land in sight. The men became discouraged.

Sailor 1: Columbus is a madman. Does he know where we are going? We're in the middle of the sea — no land anywhere!

Sailor 2: Let's speak to him.

Sailor 1: Turn back, Columbus, turn back ! The men want to turn back. There is nothing but water, water, water. We are lost!

Sailor 2: Columbus, the men are sick and tired and angry. We have little food left. What if we run out of food? What then?

Columbus: Take heart, men! We are almost there. A few more days and we will reach the Indies. Do not give up, men! We are almost there!

Narrator: And three days later, on October 12, 1492, they saw land.

Chorus: Tierra, Tierra,
There is land!
Look ahead,
Beautiful, wonderful land!
Tierra, tierra!
Tierra bonita!

Sailor 1: Thank God, thank God, we made it! Our journey is over!

Narrator: They sailed to a beautiful, small island. Columbus was sure he had reached the Indies. He had, instead, reached an island in the Bahamas. He named it San Salvador.

Columbus: Men, let's get off these ships. Let's put on our best clothes and greet the people of this land. Let's kneel and thank God we are alive.

Narrator: In the meantime, the native people looked in wonder at what they saw.

Indian 1: *(hiding behind some trees)* Look, three boats! And white men! What do they want? Why are they here?

Indian 2: They're getting off. Look, they're kissing the ground! Their leader is planting a flag. Let's go down and welcome them.

Indian 1: Welcome, friends! Welcome to our island. We come in peace. What is it that you are looking for?

Columbus: We, too, come in peace. We give these beads as a gift for your chief. Please take us to him. We come looking for gold for the Queen of Spain!

Narrator: Columbus called these people Indians because he thought he was in the Indies. They were friendly people who helped Columbus and his crew. They took him to other islands looking for gold, but there was little to be found.

Chorus: He forced the Indians
To work very hard
In a difficult search
For precious gold.

Narrator: After seven months on the island, Columbus decided to return to Spain. Forty men stayed behind to build a fort and Christianize the Natives.

Columbus: It's time to go back. We'll take back what we found here — gold, some birds, and some native people. These people will make good servants for the court.

Chorus: Columbus, Columbus,
Took what he wanted
For the Queen of Spain.
Was he a hero?
Maybe a tyrant?
What do you think
Columbus was?
What do you think
Columbus was?

Narrator: Columbus returned to Spain as a hero. Queen Isabella welcomed him and made him Governor of all the lands in the new world. He made three more trips, but it was his first that was most important because it opened up the New World.

Halloween

Halloween is celebrated on October 31. It is not a legal holiday. Originally, it was a festival for the dead. Over the years it has become a special evening for children. They put on costumes and go from house to house asking for treats — usually candy. Adults also like to put on costumes and go to parties.

Prepare for the play. Listen and write.

People like _____

_____

_____

_____

_____

_____

_____

Background Reading for the Play

This is the story of a young schoolmaster, Ichabod Crane. He comes to a small village in the Valley of Sleepy Hollow to work as a teacher.

The people of this village like to spend their evenings telling stories, especially stories about ghosts. Their favorite is "The Headless Horseman," who rides the countryside every night looking for his head!

Everything goes well for Ichabod. Life is good there, and he has met Katrina Van Tassel, the daughter of a very rich farmer. He dreams about marrying her.

One evening at a party, he proposes marriage. But Katrina refuses. She wants to marry Brom Bones, a strong, handsome man. He likes to play jokes on people, and he doesn't like Ichabod.

Katrina's refusal upsets Ichabod. That evening while he is going home from the party at her house, something terrible happens. He is chased by the Headless Horseman! The Horseman throws his head at Ichabod!

From that night on, Ichabod is never seen again. Some people think that the Headless Horseman took poor Ichabod away. Others are not so sure. What do you think happened?

Answer

1. Ichabod Crane was a _____.

2. "The _____Horseman" is a _____story.

3. The horseman rides at night looking for his _____.

4. Ichabod wanted to _____ Katrina.

5. Katrina is the _____ of a very rich _____.

6. Katrina _____ to marry Ichabod.

7. The headless horseman _____ Ichabod.

8. The horseman _____ his head at Ichabod.

Pronounce

village	countryside	superstition
valley	schoolmaster	Sleepy Hollow
shadow	townspeople	headless horseman
haunted	beautiful	invitation
pumpkin	talented	
		humiliation

left his grave	looking for his head	needed extra money
came to town	teaching their children	continued with the lesson
came to our home	talked to my father	loved his farm
get rid of this fellow	dancing with Katrina	headed for home

Match

1. _____ A valley   A. has many skills.

2. _____ A superstition   B. to a party.

3. _____ The countryside   C. teaches school.

4. _____ The headless horseman   D. is a place between two hills.

5. _____ A schoolmaster   E. has ghosts in it.

6. _____ Townspeople   F. is a village.

7. _____ A talented person   G. is a rider without a head.

8. _____ I have an invitation   H. is a belief in ghosts or magic.

9. _____ A humiliated person   I. is the area around a village.

10. _____ A haunted house.   J. feels foolish and stupid.

11. _____ Sleepy Hollow   K. live in a town.

Copy and say

1. A valley _____

2. _____

3. _____

4. _____

5. _____

6. _____

7. _____

8. _____

9. _____

10. _____

11. _____

COMING SOON
A HALLOWEEN SPECTACULAR!

The Headless Horseman Rides Again

Hoofbeats thunder across the bridge.
With terror in his heart, Ichabod turns and runs.
Will he escape the headless horseman?

Talk about the poster.

The ESL Playhouse

PRESENTS

The Headless Horseman Rides Again

Adapted from "The Legend of Sleepy Hollow"
by Washington Irving

PRODUCED BY _____

DIRECTED BY _____

THE CAST

Narrator _____

Ichabod Crane _____

Katrina Van Tassel _____

Brom Bones _____

Chorus _____

_____

_____

_____

TIME: 1800s

PLACE: Tarrytown, a small village in Sleepy Hollow in New York State

STORY: A nervous schoolmaster is scared by a strange horseman.

Your Playbill

The Headless Horseman Rides Again

Narrator: Once upon a time, there was a small village in the valley of Sleepy Hollow. It was a sleepy little town full of superstitions and unusual stories. People said that very strange things happened in Sleepy Hollow.

Chorus: What was strange?
What was so strange?
In that Valley
Of Sleepy Hollow?

Narrator: Well, people said they could hear voices with nobody around.
And, of course, everyone knew about the ghost which haunted that region.

Chorus: A ghost! A Ghost!
Tell us! Tell us
About the Ghost!
Tell us! Tell us!
About the ghost!

Narrator: Every night the ghost left his grave and rode through the countryside looking for his head! That's right! A ghost looking for his head! He was called the Headless Horseman!

Chorus: They told this story
Again and again!
About the Ghost
Looking for his head!
About the Ghost
Looking for his head!

Narrator: Then, one day a new schoolmaster came to town. He was a thin, nervous fellow. Listen:

Ichabod: The townspeople gave me this position, and I soon began teaching their children. It was hard work, and the pay was poor.

Chorus: Hard work, hard work!
And little pay!
Hard work, hard work!
With little pay!

Ichabod: I needed extra money. So, I began to give the young ladies of the village singing lessons after school. After the lessons, I would stay and talk with the men. Often, I went home late at night.

Chorus: Were you scared?
Were you scared?
Walking all alone?
In the dark of the night?
In the dead of the night?

Ichabod: O yes, all those shadows and strange noises at night. I walked fast!

Narrator: But he continued with the lessons. He loved giving lessons, especially to one beautiful young woman, Katrina Van Tassel.

Ichabod: Ah! Katrina Van Tassel! She was beautiful; she was talented. And she came from a rich family. And I wanted nothing more than to marry her and be rich, too.

Katrina: Ichabod came to our home very often. He was a strange looking fellow. He often talked to my father. I think he loved my father's farm more than anything.

Ichabod: I dreamed only one thing: making Katrina my wife.

Narrator: But there was a problem. His name was Brom Bones, a handsome young man and the strongest in the village; and he loved Katrina, too.

Brom Bones: Katrina is mine! I love her, and she loves me. I'll get rid of this fellow, this Ichabod Crane. He will leave Sleepy Hollow forever!

Chorus: Both love Katrina.
Which will she choose?
Which will she choose?

Narrator: One day, an invitation arrived for a party at the Van Tassel farm. The whole village was invited – Ichabod and Brom Bones, too.

Ichabod: I let the children go home early from school so that I could shave, wash, and look my the best for the party. I wanted to ask Katrina to marry me that night!

Narrator: It is now evening at the Van Tassel party. People are eating, drinking, singing, and dancing.

Brom Bones: *(enters angrily)* There he is again, Ichabod, dancing with my Katrina. You'll pay for this, Ichabod Crane. You'll pay for this! You can't take my girl away from me!

Narrator: Every chance he got, Ichabod danced with Katrina! Finally, he got her aside to ask her a very important question.

Ichabod: Katrina, I want to ask you to be my wife. I love you! Will you marry me?

Katrina: *(very surprised)* Oh, I don't know, Ichabod, I just don't know. *(She runs away from him.)* No, Ichabod, no!

Ichabod: *(Shocked and embarassed)* What humiliation! This is too much for me! I must leave at once! I must leave! I want to go home as quickly as possible.

Narrator: He ran out the door, got on his horse, and headed for home, tired, confused, angry. Suddenly, he heard something!

Ichabod: Who's that? What's that? Is it the wind? Is it the trees? What is it? I hear something. Ah! And I think I see something. It's coming after me! Oh, my God, something is chasing me!

Chorus: Sure enough!
Sure enough!
Someone or something
Was chasing him!
Someone or something
Was chasing him!
Chasing him!

Ichabod: Oh, no! Oh, no! It can't be! But it is! It's the Headless Horseman. The Headless Horseman is chasing me!

Chorus: The Headless Horseman
Was chasing him.
With a head in his hand.
A head in his hand.
Imagine that!
A head in his hand.

Narrator: Just then, the Headless Horseman threw something at Ichabod. It looked like a head. It was a head!

Ichabod: Oh no! Not a head! I'll run away and never come back!

Chorus: Run, Ichabod, run!
Run, Ichabod, run!
Run from the Horseman,
Run, run, run!

Narrator: The next day, Ichabod was gone! He was nowhere to be seen. They found only his horse. Beside it was a smashed pumpkin.

Katrina: *(smiling)* Really, Bones, you shouldn't do such terrible things. Poor, poor Ichabod!

Brom Bones: *(smiling)* That wasn't me. That was the Headless Horseman riding again!

Narrator: They laughed and laughed. Soon after, they got married, and poor, poor Ichabod was never, ever seen again in the valley of Sleepy Hollow.

Veterans Day

Veterans are men and women who have served in the military during times of war. Veterans Day is on November 11. Originally, it was called Armistice Day to mark the end of World War I. On that day in 1918, the "the war to end all wars" ended. In 1954, it was changed to Veterans Day to honor the veterans of all America's wars.

Prepare for the play. Listen and write.

America has had many wars

_____

_____

_____

_____

_____

_____

_____

Background Reading for the Play

June 6, 1944, is the date of the largest invasion in history. The invasion, called Operation Overlord,was the turning point of World War II in Europe. The exact date of the invasion was secret. It was simply called D-day. General Dwight D. Eisenhower was the commander of the invasion army. The army was led by American, British, and Canadian forces. They were called the allies.

The German army knew that the Allies were going to attack. So they fortified the coast of France. Their fortifications were called the Atlantic Wall and were meant to stop the invasion. Throughout the spring of 1944, air photos and spies told the Germans that a huge number of men and machines were in England, right across the English Channel.

Then they waited and waited. They knew that Eisenhower needed good weather to get across the channel. He looked for an opportunity to attack. Finally, it came on June 6. The day began with heavy rain and strong winds, but sixteen hours of good weather was predicted, and Eisenhower gave the order to attack.

In the meantime, Erwin Rommel, the German commander, decided to go back to Germany for his wife's birthday. He was sure that Eisenhower would not plan an invasion in such bad weather. It was too risky. But that's exactly what happened.

Answer

1. June 6, 1944 is the date of the _____ of Europe.

2. General Eisenhower was the _____ of the invasion army.

3. The American, British and Canadian forces were called the _____.

4. The Germans fortified the coast of _____.

5. Air _____ and _____ told the Germans that there were many men

   and machines across the English _____.

6. On June 6, the day began with heavy _____ and strong _____.

7. However, sixteen hours of good _____ was predicted.

8. Rommel was sure Eisenhower would not _____ in bad weather.

9. Rommel went to _____ for his wife's _____.

10. Operation Overlord was the largest invasion in _____.

Pronounce

battle	occupy	prepare	invasion	opportunity
vital	fortify	secure	decision	
	penetrate	postpone		
	miserable			
	liberate			

it's coming very soon	it's top secret	it's difficult
we'll surprise them	it's not a good time	we'll act now
they're eager to go	they're ready to go	we'll get the job done
they'll attack soon	it's a good time	I'm very proud

Match

1. _____ A battle   A. is a chance.

2. _____ The invasion   B. is to get ready.

3. _____ The Germans   C. is to be safe.

4. _____ To prepare   D. is a fight in a war.

5. _____ To fortify   E. is very important.

6. _____ The Allies   F. was on D-Day.

7. _____ Vital   G. penetrated the Atlantic Wall.

8. _____ An opportunity   H. is to be very uncomfortable.

9. _____ Eisenhower   I. occupied France.

10. _____ To be miserable   J. is to make something strong.

11. _____ To be secure   K. is to make free.

12. _____ To liberate   L. made the decision.

Copy and say

1. A battle _____

2. _____

3. _____

4. _____

5. _____

6. _____

7. _____

8. _____

9. _____

10. _____

11. _____

12. _____

This Week Only
for Veterans Day

D–Day

The Largest Invasion in History

*Everyone knows an invasion is coming,
but when and where will the Allies strike?
Thousands of lives and the future of Europe
hang in the balance!*

Talk about the poster.

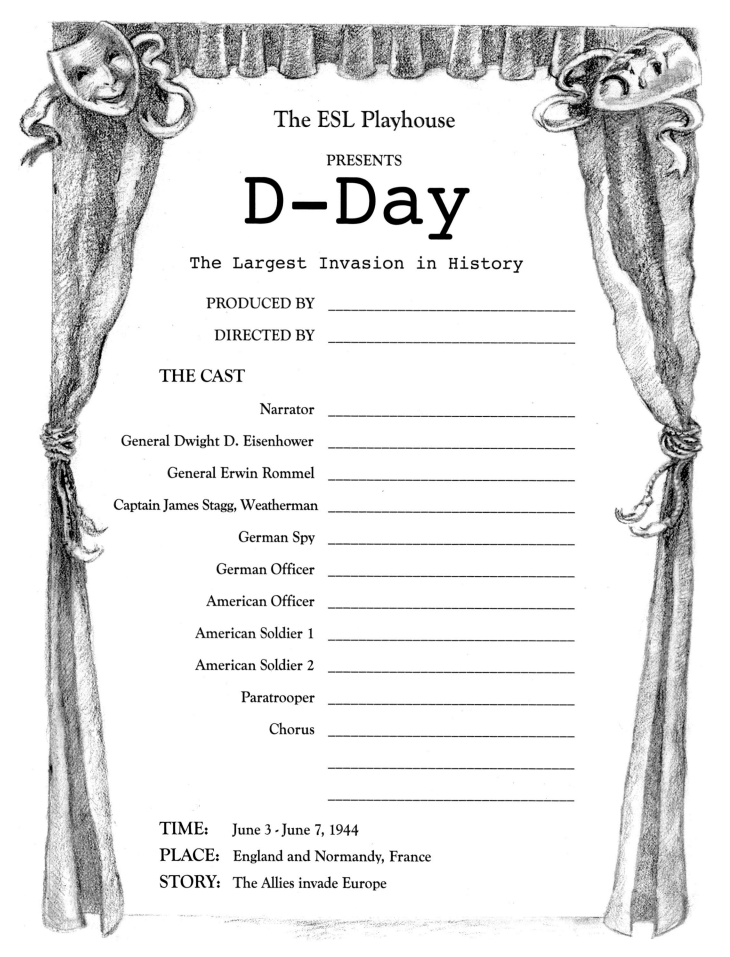

The ESL Playhouse

PRESENTS

D-Day

The Largest Invasion in History

PRODUCED BY   _____

DIRECTED BY   _____

THE CAST

Narrator   _____

General Dwight D. Eisenhower   _____

General Erwin Rommel   _____

Captain James Stagg, Weatherman   _____

German Spy   _____

German Officer   _____

American Officer   _____

American Soldier 1   _____

American Soldier 2   _____

Paratrooper   _____

Chorus   _____

_____

_____

TIME: June 3 - June 7, 1944

PLACE: England and Normandy, France

STORY: The Allies invade Europe

D-Day

Narrator: The war in Europe is almost over. There is one more major battle ahead, the invasion of France. The German army is occupying most of Europe. The Allies must invade. That is the only way the war in Europe will end. The Allies have been preparing for the invasion for over a year. The Germans know it is coming. But when? Where?

Chorus: They don't know when.
They don't know where.
The invasion is coming.
It's coming very soon.
They know it's coming,
But when and where?

Eisenhower: We must keep our plans top secret. If this invasion is to be successful, we must keep it top secret. No one is to know when or where we will land.

Captain Stagg: Yes sir. It's top secret. But it's difficult. There are spies everywhere. And we know their airplanes are taking pictures.

Narrator: On the other side of the Atlantic, in France, a German spy is talking to Rommel.

German Spy: We have secret information that the Allies will leave from Dover, England. They are building up troops there. We have photos of this. They will go from Dover to Calais. This is where they will land.

Rommel: *(looking at the photos)* Hmm, that's what it looks like—Calais, the shortest distance between England and France. We will prepare to meet them at Calais. Now, we must continue to fortify the seacoast. We must continue to build an Atlantic Wall that no one can penetrate.

Chorus: The Germans placed their guns
Along the coast of France.
They built their concrete forts
Along the coast of France,
They fortified the cliffs
At Calais and Normandy
Along the coast of France.

Eisenhower: You know, Rommel expects us in Calais. Let him think that, but we'll surprise him in Normandy. Captain Stagg, how does the weather look for June 3?

Captain Stagg: General, the weather report is bad. The sea is rough and the winds are high. It's not a good time for ships at sea or for a landing.

Eisenhower: If we postpone the invasion much longer, the Germans will find out our secrets. We cannot wait much longer. We must catch them by surprise. This is vital! There are spies everywhere. We must act very soon, as soon as the weather breaks.

Chorus: Waiting, waiting,
You lose much time.
Much can happen
While you wait.
Wait no longer,
Wait no longer!

Narrator: On June 5, Eisenhower meets with some of his officers.

Eisenhower: How's the weather, Captain?

Captain Stagg: The sea is rough now, but it looks like there will be 16 hours of good weather tomorrow.

Eisenhower: Then we'll act now! We will not miss this opportunity! Men, this it it. We can wait no longer. The sea is rough, but the moon is full, and the rain is sure to stop. Gentlemen, the decision is made. Tell your men June 6 is D-Day. We invade tomorrow!

American Officer: Yes sir! Excellent news, General! Our men have been ready and waiting for weeks. They don't like waiting and waiting. They're eager to go. They're ready to go.

Narrator: Later, Eisenhower meets with the paratroopers.

Eisenhower: Gentlemen you will be the first to go. You will be dropped behind enemy lines. You will guide the others as they come through the Wall. That is your mission!

Paratrooper: Don't worry, general. We'll get the job done. You can count on us.

Eisenhower: Good luck and God speed. Now, go get 'em!

Paratroooper: All right, men. You heard the general. Let's go!

Narrator: Meanwhile Rommel sits in his tent thinking about the war.

Rommel: Well, we can be sure of one thing. Eisenhower will not invade in this miserable weather. We have days, maybe weeks before he attacks.

German Officer: Yes, only a fool would attack in such weather!

Rommel: I believe I shall visit my wife. It's her birthday. Besides, I really need to go to Germany. I need to see Hitler about more defense.

Chorus: Rommel, Rommel,
Your spies are wrong.
Your spies are wrong.
They will attack
They will attack
They'll attack while
You're away

Rommel: Perhaps you could take some time off, too!

German Officer: Thank you general. It's a good time to take a break.

Narrator: Then at daybreak on June 6, the largest invasion in history began. Nine-thousand airplanes filled the sky. There were five thousand ships. One hundred fifty thousand men. But securing the beach was not easy. The Germans were fortified high on a cliff. At Omaha Beach the Americans were down below.

Chorus: Nine thousand planes,
Five thousand ships,
Thousands of men,
And twenty-four hours
Of living hell.
Twenty-four hours
Of living hell!

American This is hell! The high cliffs! The mines on the beaches! The confusion!
Soldier 1: This is madness! This is hell!

Narrator: At Omaha Beach, especially, things were not going well at all. Boats were sinking and men were dying.

American We need help! We need back up! We need more men. Where are the
Soldier 2: others? Where are the others?

American Look, there! More troops, more planes, more ships are coming! Let's go!
Soldier 1: Let's go! Let's climb these bloody cliffs!

Narrator: Finally, after twenty-four hours of brutal fighting, the Allied forces of American, British, and Canadian soldiers broke through the Atlantic Wall. They secured the beaches and climbed the cliffs. Months later they marched into Paris.

Chorus: They secured the beach
And liberated France.
Americans, Canadians,
British soldiers
Led the way.
Europe was free,
Free at last!

Narrator: Twenty years later, Eisenhower visited Normandy again.

Eisenhower: In one day alone, we lost 20,000 men, a terrible, terrible price. These men died so that the world could be free. It shows what free men will do. I am very proud of these brave men. We owe everything to our veterans.

Thanksgiving

Thanksgiving was made a national holiday in 1863. It is celebrated on the fourth Thursday in November. It celebrates the first harvest in the New World by European settlers. Nowadays, families carry on the tradition by enjoying a big turkey dinner together. It is one of the biggest travel times of the year as families come together from all over the country.

Prepare for the play. Listen and write.

In 1620,

_____

_____

_____

_____

_____

_____

_____

Background Reading for the Play

In 1620, a group of men and women called Pilgrims came to this country for religious freedom. One hundred and one Pilgrims from England arrived on Cape Cod in Massachusetts in the cold month of November.

The journey was not easy. They had traveled sixty-six days in a small boat, the Mayflower. During the journey, one person died and another was born. When they arrived, a group of friendly Indians welcomed them. The Pilgrims and the Indians agreed to not make war. Both groups wanted peace.

The first winter was terrible. There was not enough food, and there was much disease. Over half the Pilgrims died. Finally, spring arrived and the Pilgrims were thankful they had survived as a community. They were ready to plant, work hard, and make a new life for themselves in the new land. One of the Indians, Squanto, gave them a lot of help and advice.

Their harvest was good that year, and they had plenty of food to eat for the winter. They invited the Indians to a big feast of thanksgiving. Ninety Indians came. There were more Indians than Pilgrims. They celebrated for three days.

Answer

1. The Pilgrims came to this country for religious _____.

2. They _____ on Cape Cod.

3. The journey was _____ days long.

4. The Indians _____ them.

5. The two groups agreed not to make _____.

6. The first winter was _____.

7. Over _____ the Pilgrims died.

8. They invited the Indians to a big _____.

9. _____ Indians came.

10. They _____ for three days.

Pronounce

pilgrim	governor	arrive	exhausted	Massasoit
harvest	fortunate	survive	delicious	
hungry	vegetable		together	
rabbit	Indian		Thanksgiving	
turkey	Mayflower			

easy to plant	good to eat	time to plant	happy to share
to make a new life	to live in peace	to hunt for deer	
sick and exhausted	tired and hungry	corn and squash	
deer and turkey	singing and games	they ate and ate	

Match

1. _____ The Pilgrims   A. are plants that can be eaten.

2. _____ A governor   B. is to be very lucky.

3. _____ To be exhausted   C. is to come to a place.

4. _____ To be fortunate   D. is to live through difficulty.

5. _____ A harvest   E. landed in Massachusetts.

6. _____ Vegetables   F. is to be very tired.

7. _____ Rabbits   G. is a leader.

8. _____ Turkeys   H. tastes very good.

9. _____ Delicious food   I. are animals with long ears.

10. _____ To arrive   J. is the time when food is collected.

11. _____ To survive   K. are large birds.

Copy and say

1. The Pilgrims _____

2. _____

3. _____

4. _____

5. _____

6. _____

7. _____

8. _____

9. _____

10. _____

11. _____

The First Thanksgiving

Squanto Helps the Pilgrims

They shared hardship and the spring planting.
They shared the harvest and the feast.
They planned to share the land.

Talk about the poster.

The Poster for the Play
Thanksgiving • 45

The ESL Playhouse

PRESENTS

The First Thanksgiving

Squanto Helps the Pilgrims'
Arrival and Survival in the New World

PRODUCED BY _____

DIRECTED BY _____

THE CAST

Narrator _____

Pilgrim 1 _____

Pilgrim 2 _____

Governor Bradford _____

Massasoit, Indian Chief _____

Squanto, Indian Friend _____

Chorus _____

_____

_____

_____

TIME: Winter, 1620 - Fall, 1621

PLACE: Cape Cod, Massachusetts

STORY: A group of people from England, called the Pilgrims, seek
religious freedom in a new land.

Your Playbill

The First Thanksgiving

Narrator: It's a very cold winter day in November, 1620. A ship, the Mayflower, is arriving. It's landing at Cape Cod, Massachusetts, and it's bringing 101 Pilgrims.

Pilgrim 1: *(excitedly)* Look! Look! Look there! I see land! Finally, land!

Pilgrim 2: *(excitedly)* I see it, too! Land! Thank God, thank God! It's been long. Sixty-six days on this small boat on the terrible, terrible sea.

Governor Bradford: Finally, our journey is over. This place will be our new home. It's a cold place — not much here, but our people are sick and exhausted, and we must stop. Thank God, we are here!

Chorus: They made it! They made it!
The Mayflower made it!
Sixty-six days on the sea.
Sixty-six days on the sea.
One person died.
A baby was born.
Sixty-six days on the sea.
Sixty-six days on the sea.

Pilgrim 1: Look, Governor! Indians!

Gov. Bradford: Greetings! We are travelers from far across the sea. We come in peace. We come in peace to make a new life for ourselves.

Massasoit: *(enters with some Indians)* Welcome, friends! We welcome you to this land. You are cold, tired, and hungry! Come, let us help you. It is too late to plant now, but in the spring we will plant together!

Narrator: They signed a pact to live in peace, not make war. The Pilgrims were very fortunate to have such good friends who helped them. But half of the Pilgrims died that first terrible winter.

Chorus: Half of the Pilgrims died.
Half of the Pilgrims died.

Narrator: Finally spring arrived. One Indian especially helped the Pilgrims. His name was Squanto.

Squanto : Friends, it is now spring and time to plant. Let me show you how. This is corn. It is easy to plant. And squash and pumpkin seeds too. They are all good to eat. And there is good fishing here.

Pilgrim 1: Thank you, Squanto. You are a good friend. You teach us everything. We will have a good harvest in the fall. And we will not go hungry.

Pilgrim 2: Without you, Squanto, I don't know what we would do.

Chorus: He taught them to plant
Corn and squash
And vegetables, too.
He taught them to fish.
He taught them to hunt
For rabbit, deer,
And turkey, too.
Rabbit, deer,
And turkey, too.

Narrator: It's now late summer. The Pilgrims are happy because the harvest has been very good and there will be much food for winter.

Gov. Bradford: Good day, my friends!

Pilgrim 1: Good day, Governor, let us show you the wonderful harvest we had this year. We will not go hungry this winter. We have much food and much to be thankful for.

Pilgrim 2: Governor, perhaps we could celebrate our harvest — have a day of feasting, and singing and games. It would be good for the village.

Chorus: A feast, a feast,
You need a feast.
It's good for the body.
It's good for the soul.
A feast, a feast,
You shall have a feast!

Gov. Bradford: Ah ! Yes, a day of celebration! An excellent idea! We will celebrate and give thanks for what we have. Our people have done well in this new land. But let's not forget our Indian friends. We must invite them, too.

Narrator: So, word got around for the big celebration. The men of the village hunted rabbit, turkey, and deer. And the women cooked and baked for days. The children helped their mothers. Days later, Massosoit arrived for the feast. He came with 90 Indians.

Massasoit: Good morning, my friends. My people and I are here for the celebration. We are ready for the feast.

Gov. Bradford: *(surprised that so many Indians came)* Welcome, welcome my friends! We are almost ready. *(Aside)* Hmm, I don't think we will have enough food. We didn't expect so many. Will there be enough for everybody?

Chorus: Squanto, Squanto!
Get more game.
Squanto, Squanto!
Get more game.
Get more food
For the feast!

Massasoit: Governor, please, I will send my best men to the forest for more turkey, deer, and rabbit. Don't worry! They will be back quickly. *(Squanto and five Indians run off stage.)*

Narrator: Everything is almost ready. *(The Pilgrim women enter with huge platters of food placing it on table and talking among themselves.)*

Gov. Bradford: Ah, ladies! It all looks wonderful and delicious. You have done well. You have worked very hard. Thank you for all you have done. And look, the Indians are back with more.

Squanto : I think this will be enough for everyone! *(Hands the game to a Pilgrim lady who takes it away.)*

Narrator: So they all sat down for the wonderful feast, happy to share it with their new friends.

Pilgrim 2: Here, Squanto, have some more. You didn't eat enough. Have some more turkey. Try the pumpkin pie. Eat! Eat!

Squanto : I had more than enough. Thank you. It is all very, very delicious. It is a good feast we are having. Very, very good! *(Pats his stomach.)*

Chorus: And so they ate
And ate and ate
For three full days
Of celebration,
Giving thanks
For what they had,
For all they had.

Narrator: So, dear friends, that was our very first Thanksgiving. Now let us, too, enjoy the food at our Thanksgiving table and give thanks for all that we have.

Chorus: Let us all give thanks
For what we have.
Let us give thanks
For all we have.
One and all!

Everybody on stage: Happy Thanksgiving, everyone!

Christmas

Christmas is celebrated on December 25. It is a Christian holiday to celebrate the birth of Christ. However, nowadays, almost everybody celebrates Christmas as a time to exchange Christmas cards and gifts. Santa Claus is the the symbol for gift giving. Children are told that Santa Claus will bring gifts Christmas Eve and leave them under the family tree.

Prepare for the play. Listen and write.

Christmas is
_____

_____

_____

_____

_____

_____

_____

Background Reading for the Play

A Christmas Carol is about a man called Scrooge. He is a man who loves money more than anything else. People are not important to him. Only money is. And Christmas is not important to him either. He doesn't celebrate Christmas. It is just another workday for him.

One night Scrooge gets a big shock. In his dreams, he is visited by three ghosts: the Ghost of Christmas Past, the Ghost of Christmas Present, and the Ghost of Christmas Future. The ghosts show him his life in the past, as it is now, and what it will be. Scrooge doesn't like what he sees. His life is cold and empty.

He is also very upset when he sees a crippled boy, Tiny Tim, the son of his clerk, Bob Cratchitt. The little boy may die.

When Scrooge wakes up, he sees the truth about his life. He decides to change and to become an unselfish and kind man. He decides to help others. And he decides to become a "second father" to Tiny Tim. In the end, Scrooge becomes a happy person who celebrates Christmas every year.

Answer

1. Scrooge loves _____.

2. He doesn't _____ Christmas.

3. Scrooge is visited in his _____.

4. The visitors are _____.

5. Scrooge's life is _____ and empty.

6. He is upset when he sees a _____ boy.

7. The little boy may _____.

8. Scrooge wakes up and sees the _____ about his life.

9. He decides to become an _____ man.

10. He becomes a second_____ for Tiny Tim.

Pronounce

Christmas	restless	celebrate	deserve
dingy	crippled	visitor	believe
nephew	selfish	suddenly	invite
partner	greedy	family	

Be off with you!	Come in early!	Be here early!
Wake up!	Come with me!	Look there!
Take me back!	Get out of here!	Go away!

Match

1. _____ A dingy room   A. is the place where dead people are buried.

2. _____ Your nephew   B. is to earn something by good work.

3. _____ Your partner   C. has a bad leg.

4. _____ A restless person   D. is a dark and cold place.

5. _____ To deserve   E. is to be unfair or steal.

6. _____ To cheat   F. is your sister or brother's son.

7. _____ A crippled person   G. shares your life or business with you.

8. _____ A cemetery   H. feels very uncomfortable.

9. _____ Selfish people   I. think only of themselves.

Copy and say

1. A dingy room _____

2. _____

3. _____

4. _____

5. _____

6. _____

7. _____

8. _____

9. _____

A Classic for Christmas!

This week ONLY

Scrooge

Based on Charles Dickens's "A Christmas Carol"

"Bah! Humbug!" said old Mr. Scrooge. "Christmas is for fools!"
But who is knocking on his door? And who visits him in the night?
It may be a dream, but old Scrooge will never be the same again!

Talk about the poster.

The ESL Playhouse

PRESENTS

Scrooge

Adapted from "A Christmas Carol"
by Charles Dickens

PRODUCED BY _____

DIRECTED BY _____

THE CAST

Narrator _____

Scrooge _____

His nephew _____

Bob Cratchit _____

Christopher Marley,
Scrooge's dead partner _____

The Ghost of Christmas Past _____

The Ghost of Christmas Present _____

The Ghost of Christmas Future _____

Chorus _____

_____

_____

_____

TIME: Christmas Eve

PLACE: London

STORY: A selfish, old man learns the true meaning of Christmas.

Scrooge

Narrator: It's Christmas Eve and Scrooge is in his cold, dingy office. He is at his desk working, working, working. His clerk, Bob Cratchit, is working at a desk behind him. Scrooge suddenly looks up. *(music offstage)*

Scrooge: What's that I hear? What is it? I heard something! What was it?

Chorus: Scrooge, Scrooge.
What are you doing?
What are you doing?
It's Christmas Eve.
It's Christmas Eve.

Scrooge: *(angry and in a bad mood)* I'm counting my money. That's what I'm doing. I'm counting my money.

Chorus: But Scrooge, Scrooge,
It's Christmas Eve!
It's time to go
And celebrate!

Scrooge: Celebrate? Bah! Humbug! I don't celebrate Christmas. Christmas is for fools. For fools!

Narrator: There is a knock on the door and his nephew enters.

Nephew: Merry Christmas, Uncle! Merry Christmas, Bob. How are you today, Uncle? I came here to invite you for Christmas dinner. Please, come!

Scrooge: Bah! Humbug! Christmas is for fools. I don't celebrate Christmas!

Nephew: But, Uncle . . .?

Scrooge: Listen, you celebrate your way, and I'll celebrate my way.

Nephew: Well, . . . all right. But if you change your mind. . .

Scrooge: I've got work to do. So, be off with you!

Nephew: Well, good bye, then. Merry Christmas, Bob!

Bob Cratchit: Merry Christmas, and to your family, too!

Scrooge: Christmas! Bah! Humbug! Now, Cratchit, don't forget. Come in early tomorrow! There's work to be done.

Bob Cratchit: But, Mr. Scrooge, tomorrow is Christmas Day! I was hoping to spend it with my family.

Scrooge: Christmas! Well, I suppose you must have it off. But the day after's a working day! So, be here early! People who celebrate Christmas are fools! See that you are here early, Cratchit. Early!

Bob Cratchit: All right, Mr. Scrooge, I will. Now, goodbye, and Merry Christmas to you!

Scrooge: Christmas! Bah! Humbug!

Narrator: Later that evening. Scrooge is sitting in the dark by the fire. He is asleep. He hears a knock on the door.

Scrooge: What's that? What's that I hear? I see something? What is it? Who is it?

Marley: It is I, your old business partner, Christopher Marley.

Scrooge: But you are dead! You died many years ago! What do you want?

Marley: Yes, I am dead, but my spirit is roaming the earth. You and I cheated many people in our business. And now my Spirit is restless and sad.

Scrooge: The people were fools! They deserved what they got!

Chorus: Scrooge, Scooge!
You cheated people,
All of the people.
You were greedy,
Very, very greedy!

Marley: Scrooge, Scrooge, tonight you will have three visitors. They will tell you about your life. Listen to them, Scrooge. Listen to them!

Ghost of Christmas Past: *(As Scrooge climbs into bed, the ghost enters)*
Wake up, Scrooge! Wake up, and come with me! Come!

Scrooge: What? Who are you? What do you want? Get out of here! Go away!

Ghost of Christmas Past:
I am the Ghost of Christmas Past. I am here to teach you a lesson, Scrooge. I am taking you back to your past life. You will see, Scrooge, everything is not money! Now, look there, in the distance. That is your past life!

Scrooge: Oh! How happy I was! Even though we had no money, I was so happy.

Ghost of Christmas Past: And do you see that lovely, young woman?

Scrooge: Ah, yes! I loved her, and she loved me. But she left me because I loved money more. Please, please, Ghost, no more! I can't look anymore.

Ghost of Christmas Past:
We are finished, Scrooge, but you will have other visitors tonight.
(Leaves and the Ghost of Christmas Present enters)

Ghost of Christmas Present:
I am the Ghost of Christmas Present. Now, Scrooge, I will show you how Christmas should be celebrated! Christmas is not for fools. It's for families! Look!

Scrooge: That's my nephew's home! They are singing and dancing. They are so happy. And over there, there's my clerk, Bob Cratchit, and his family. They are celebrating, too! But who's that little boy?

Ghost of Christmas Present:
That's his son, Tiny Tim. He's crippled! He can't walk! They don't have money for doctors. Tiny Tim may die.

Scrooge: Oh, no! Take me back! Take me back! I can't look anymore! No more, please!

Ghost of Christmas Present:
You will have one more visitor, Scrooge, one more visitor!

Ghost of Christmas Future:
(enters) Scrooge! Scrooge! Come with me! I am the ghost of Christmas Future. I will show you what your future will be. Look!

Scrooge: That's a cemetery! Somebody died! Who is it? It looks like me!

Ghost of Christmas Future:
>It is you, Scrooge. It is you. You are dead! They are burying you! Listen, listen to what they are saying about you.

Chorus: Scrooge, old Scrooge
Was a selfish man,
Greedy and selfish,
Selfish and greedy.
Did he ever, ever
Help anyone?
No, never, never!
And now he's dead
Forever and ever!
(They laugh!)

Scrooge: Oh no! Oh, no! I'm dead, dead and forgotten. But what happened to Tiny Tim? Where is he? I don't see him!

Ghost of Christmas Future: Tiny Tim is also dead!

Scrooge: That little boy dead! I can't believe it! Dear Ghost, tell me. Do you think we can change the future? Can the future be changed? Is it possible?

Ghost of Christmas Future:
>Only if we change the present, Scrooge. Only if we change the present. The present can change the future.

Narrator: Scrooge awakens the next morning from a deep, deep sleep. It's Christmas Day.

Scrooge: What a strange dream I had! What day is it? Why, it's Christmas Day! Wonderful! I have much to do! First, I will send Cratchit a huge Christmas turkey for his hungry family, and then I am going to give him a raise, too! Next, I'll go to my nephew's house for Christmas dinner! That will surprise him! And finally! I must give away all this money! *(Throws bills into the air.)* It's Christmas Day, and I'm going to celebrate!

Narrator: And celebrate he did. Scrooge became a changed man. Tiny Tim did not die. And Scrooge became a "second father" to him.

Chorus: Merry Christmas, Scrooge!
Merry Christmas, all!
Merry Christmas, everyone!
To family, friends and all.

New Year's Day

The celebration of the New Year actually begins on New Year's Eve, December 31. People attend parties, big and small, and wait for midnight. At 12:00, the New Year begins. People drink a toast, cheer, hug, kiss, and make noise. Many people make promises, called New Year's Resolutions, to make changes in their lives.

Prepare for the play. Listen and write.

On New Year's Eve,

_____

_____

_____

_____

_____

_____

_____

Background Reading for the Play

New Year's Eve in Times Square in New York City is world famous. It takes place in the heart of New York City every year. Thousands of people come from all over the US and the world to see the old year go out and the new year come in.

During the evening, there is continuous entertainment. There is music and dancing. Giant puppets perform. Men and women in bright red uniforms distribute flags, balloons, and the famous Times Square confetti bags.

The most important event of the evening is the lowering of the ball at midnight. This has been a tradition since 1907. Millions of people all over the world watch it on TV, and thousands of people come to New York to see it.

The ball is beautiful. It is huge, six feet in diameter, and weighs over 1,000 pounds. It is covered with small pieces of glass. Inside are hundreds of bright, colored lights.

One minute before midnight, the ball begins to come down slowly. Everyone joins in the fun as the crowd begins to count the last ten seconds before midnight and the ball begins to flash. Then everyone shouts, "Happy New Year!" Everyone hugs, kisses, blows horns, and throws confetti. There are fireworks, and a big sign suddenly appears. It shows the numerals of the new year for the first time. New Year's Eve in Times Square is quite a show!

Answer

1. Times Square is in _____.

2. _____ of people visit Times Square on New Year's Eve.

3. There is _____ entertainment.

4. People come to see the ball _____ at midnight.

5. Millions of people _____ it on TV.

6. The ball _____ over 1,000 pounds.

7. People count the last ten _____ of the old year.

8. People throw _____.

9. A new sign suddenly _____.

10. It shows the _____ of the new year.

Pronounce

reporter	festivities	decoration	1,000,000
impression	experience		300,000
confetti	historian	pandemonium	6:30
excitement	diameter		12:00
	humanity		1904
			11:59

people of all cultures	all over the U.S.	all this humanity
all the way	all the lights	all the time
all kinds of people	all waiting for the ball	
how did it all happen	the numbers are all lighted	

Match

1. _____ A reporter   A. means all the people of the earth.

2. _____ Festivities   B. is the distance through the middle.

3. _____ To experience   C. is your opinion about something.

4. _____ Humanity   D. is a lively condition.

5. _____ Your impression   E. are events in a celebration.

6. _____ A decoration   F. is a person who writes or tells the news.

7. _____ Confetti   G. is a wild and crazy celebration

8. _____ A historian   H. is little pieces of paper thrown in the air.

9. _____ The diameter   I. is to be involved in an event.

10. _____ Excitement   J. studies history.

11. _____ Pandemonium   K. makes something pretty or colorful.

Copy and say

1. _____

2. _____

3. _____

4. _____

5. _____

6. _____

7. _____

8. _____

9. _____

10. _____

11. _____

TONIGHT ONLY
AT THE ESL PLAYHOUSE

HAPPY NEW YEAR!

**And Now,
Live from New York City,
The Lowering of the Ball
At Times Square!**

Talk about the poster.

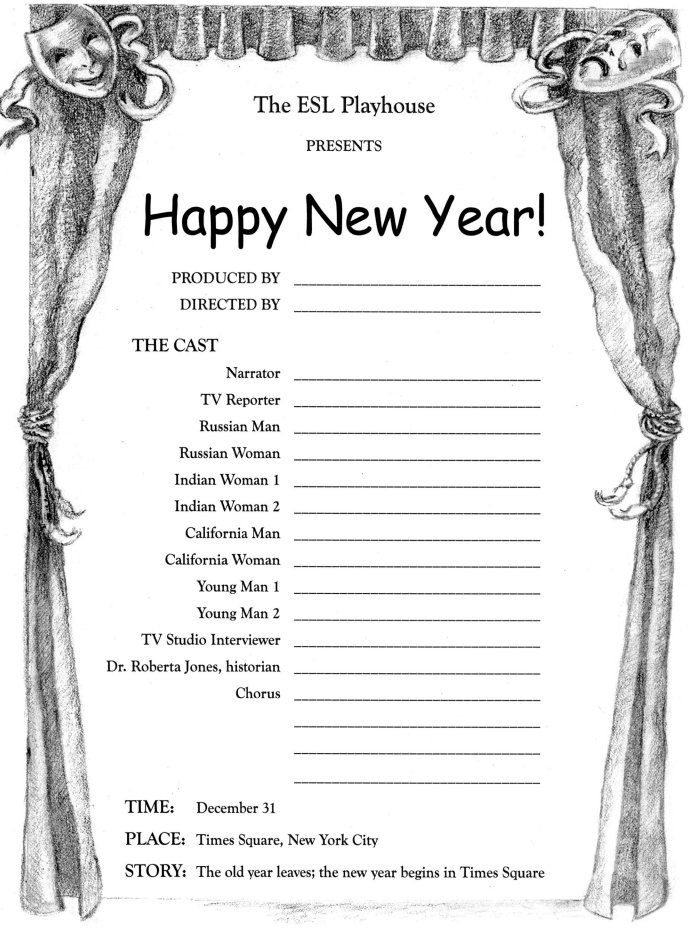

The ESL Playhouse

PRESENTS

Happy New Year!

PRODUCED BY _____

DIRECTED BY _____

THE CAST

Narrator _____

TV Reporter _____

Russian Man _____

Russian Woman _____

Indian Woman 1 _____

Indian Woman 2 _____

California Man _____

California Woman _____

Young Man 1 _____

Young Man 2 _____

TV Studio Interviewer _____

Dr. Roberta Jones, historian _____

Chorus _____

_____

_____

_____

TIME: December 31

PLACE: Times Square, New York City

STORY: The old year leaves; the new year begins in Times Square

Your Playbill

HAPPY NEW YEAR!

Narrator: From the very beginning, people of all cultures have celebrated the New Year. They celebrate in many different ways. For example, Moslems wear new clothes, Southeast Asians release birds and turtles for good luck, and the Japanese prepare rice cakes.

Chorus: What about Americans?
How do they celebrate?
Where do they celebrate
New Year's Eve?
New Year's Day?

Narrator: In America, there's always a New Year's Eve celebration in Times Square in New York City. It is so famous that people come from all over the U. S. and the world to take part in it. And millions of people watch it on TV, too.

Chorus: Three hundred thousand
Three hundred thousand
Come to Times Square
Come to Times Square
On New Year's Eve!
On New Year's Eve!

Narrator: Now, let's talk to a reporter who is at Times Square and can tell us what is going on tonight.

TV Reporter: Ladies and gentlemen, it is now 6:30 PM. Already thousands are here. They want to get here early for the festivities. They want to make sure that they get a good place to see the most important event of all — the lowering of the ball at midnight.

Chorus: The lowering of a Ball,
A huge Ball, a glass Ball,
A lighted Ball, high on a pole
Ready to fall, ready to fall
At twelve o'clock sharp!
At twelve o'clock sharp!

TV Reporter: Ladies and gentlemen, the mood this evening is a happy one. There are people from many different places. Let's talk to some. Here's a happy couple. Young man, where are you from?

New Year's Day • 67

Russian Man:	Oh, we are from Russia. We are visiting relatives in the United States. We wanted to come here, especially on New Year's Eve.
Russian Woman:	We have seen the New Year's Eve celebration on TV so we wanted to see it in person.
TV Reporter:	What have you seen so far?
Russian Woman:	Well, just a little while ago we saw them raise that beautiful ball. Everybody clapped and cheered. Everything so exciting – excuse me, is so exciting!
TV Reporter:	Well, thank you, and enjoy the rest of the evening! And now I see two women wearing saris. Ladies, where are you from?
Indian Woman 1:	We are from India. We are students at Columbia University.
Indian Woman 2:	We just finished our exams and thought it would be interesting to experience a little American culture.
TV Reporter:	How do you like it so far?
Indian Woman 1:	Oh, we're enjoying it very much. The people are very friendly, the music is wonderful. There's something going on every hour. But, it's easy to get lost in all this humanity!
TV Reporter:	Well, thank you very much. And now we have a family here.
TV Reporter:	First, where are you folks from?
California Man:	We are from California.
TV Reporter:	Really, all the way from California. And what brings you here?
California Man:	I have a brother who lives in New Jersey. We're visiting him and his family over the holidays. So we thought we would spend New Year's Eve in Times Square.
TV Reporter:	And what's your impression?
California Woman:	We love it. We love all the lights and decorations, the music. They have something going on all the time. Why, just a little while ago, they passed out these American flags, balloons and confetti.

TV Reporter: Sounds like you're having a good time.

California Man: We certainly are.

TV Reporter: And finally, we have two young men. Mind if we ask you some questions?

Young Man 1: Sure, man, no problem! What's up?

TV Reporter: Well, first, where are you guys from? You seem to be having a good time.

Young Man 2: Brooklyn. We're from Brooklyn. Yeah, we're having a blast. Lots of cool chicks here.

Young Man 1: Yeah. Cool. Really cool! Man, this place is amazing!

TV Reporter: So, there you have it! All kinds of people here at Times Square, and all waiting for that final moment when the Ball comes down at midnight. Now, let's go back to the studio.

Studio Interviewer: Thank you. Times Square sure sounds like a lot of fun. Here in the studio we have a Times Square historian, Dr. Roberta Jones, with us. Welcome to the show, Dr. Jones.

Dr. Jones: Thanks. My pleasure.

Studio Interviewer: Dr. Jones, when did this Times Square celebration begin? How did it all happen?

Dr. Jones: Well, the first celebration was in 1904. It was on the rooftop of the building called One Times Square. The New York Times, the famous newspaper, had just moved to this location, Times Square, and wanted to celebrate.

Studio Interviewer: Interesting! And how did they celebrate?

Dr. Jones: At first, they only had fireworks from the top of the building. The Ball lowering tradition didn't start until 1907.

Studio Interviewer: Really? Now tell us a little about that famous Ball.

Dr. Jones: Well, it's six feet in diameter and weighs about 1,000 pounds. Inside are hundreds of lights. On the outside are tiny bits of crystal. It really is a beautiful thing.

Studio Interviewer: It certainly is. Thank you, Dr. Jones, for telling us a little about the history of this celebration. Now back to you at Times Square. It's getting close to midnight everybody!

TV Reporter: Right you are! It's almost midnight, and the excitement is growing. All eyes are on the Ball. Folks, it's one minute before midnight! Look, the Ball is coming down!

Narrator: Now it is ten seconds to midnight. Everybody, count!

Chorus: Ten, nine, eight,
Seven, six, five,
Four, three, two,
One!
Happy New Year, everyone!
Happy New Year!
The old year is gone!
The new year is here!

TV Reporter: It's pandemonium! Everybody is hugging, kissing, blowing horns, throwing confetti!

Russian Woman: Look! A new sign with the numbers of the New Year, all lighted — and the sky full of color. What a great show!

Narrator: Well, ladies and gentlemen, this is New Year's Eve in Times Square in New York—a great party and a great celebration. Happy New Year!

Everybody: Should old acquaintance be forgot
And never brought to mind?
Should old acquaintance be forgot
And days of Auld Lang Syne?

For Auld Lang Syne, my dear,
For Auld Lang Syne,
We'll take a cup of kindness yet,
For Auld Lang Syne.
  (repeat last verse)

Martin Luther King, Jr.'s Birthday

Dr. Martin Luther King, Jr., was the leader of the Civil Rights
Movement in America. He worked for equal rights for all people,
especially America's Blacks. He was born on January 15, 1929.
His birthday is the newest national holiday. It was established in 1983.
In celebrating the day, many schools do special things to recognize
the history and progress of Black people in America.

Prepare for the play. Listen and write.

In 1955, _____

_____

_____

_____

_____

_____

_____

Background Reading for the Play

For many years there was a very serious problem in America. It was called segregation. That means that Black people and White people were separated. It was the law in the southern states. It was unfair and unconstitutional, but in the South it was the law. Black people had to live in a special part of town. They could not go to white schools or white restaurants, and they had to sit in the back of the bus. And if they protested, they were put in jail.

Dr. Martin Luther King, a popular minister and black leader, protested these terrible laws. And so did Rosa Parks. One day, very tired from a long day at work, she decided to sit at the front of the bus. The bus driver told her to move. She refused. He called the police, and she was put in jail.

The black community was angry. They met to discuss how to protest the unfair laws that made them second-class citizens. They decided that the best way was to boycott the buses. They would not ride the buses until the law was changed. They would walk, bicycle, and carpool to work, but they would not ride the buses.

Of course, the bus companies lost money carrying only a few passengers. Finally, after eight long months, the law was changed. But the fight against segregation was not over. It took many more marches and protests. In 1964, Congress passed the Civil Rights Bill, giving all people equality and ending segregation.

Answer

1. _____ was a very serious problem in America.

2. It was the law in the _____ states.

3. Black people lived in a special part of _____.

4. They had to sit in the _____ of the bus.

5. If they _____ they were put in jail.

6. One day, Rosa Parks was very _____. She sat at the _____.

7. The _____ _____ told her to move.

8. The Black community decided to _____ the buses.

9. With only a few _____, the bus company lost _____.

10. In 1964, Congress _____ the Civil Rights Bill.

Pronounce

trouble	community	segregation	violence
boycott	incredible	transportation	terrible
bankrupt	equality	conversation	wonderful
justice		discrimination	history

you don't belong here	I'm not moving	Don't move, Rosa
don't make trouble	she won't sit in the back	I'm not going to the back
don't ride the buses	we won't take the bus	it won't be easy
this can't continue	I wouldn't go to the back	I wasn't going to move

Match

1. _____ To make trouble   A. means to refuse to buy or use.

2. _____ A community   B. is the opposite of peace.

3. _____ An incredible thing   C. wanted justice.

4. _____ Discrimination   D. is to separate.

5. _____ To boycott   E. is to create a problem.

6. _____ Violence   F. is to have the same rights.

7. _____ To segregate   G. is not having equal rights.

8. _____ The buses   H. were going bankrupt.

9. _____ The Blacks   I. is difficult to believe.

10. _____ Equality   J. is a group of people.

Copy and say

To make trouble

1. _____

2. _____

3. _____

4. _____

5. _____

6. _____

7. _____

8. _____

9. _____

10. _____

COMING IN JANUARY

Boycott!

The Rosa Parks Story

In Montgomery, Alabama,
Rosa Parks would not move to the back of the bus.
Doctor Martin Luther King, Jr., organized their community,
and brought their city to its knees.

Talk about the poster.

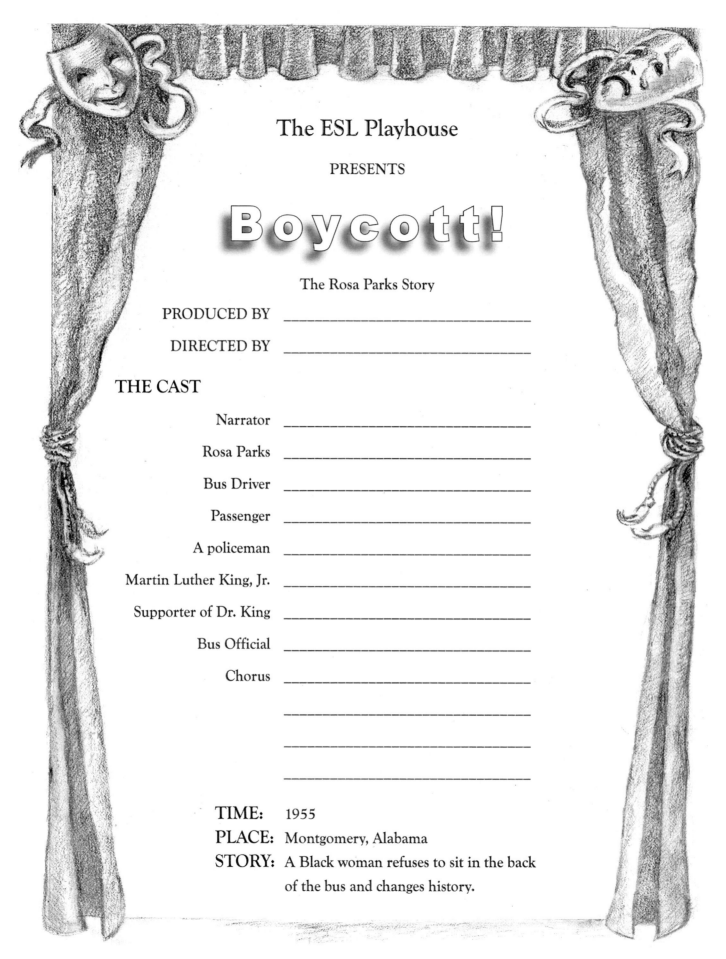

The ESL Playhouse

PRESENTS

Boycott!

The Rosa Parks Story

PRODUCED BY _____

DIRECTED BY _____

THE CAST

Narrator _____

Rosa Parks _____

Bus Driver _____

Passenger _____

A policeman _____

Martin Luther King, Jr. _____

Supporter of Dr. King _____

Bus Official _____

Chorus _____

_____

_____

_____

TIME: 1955
PLACE: Montgomery, Alabama
STORY: A Black woman refuses to sit in the back
of the bus and changes history.

Boycott!

Narrator: Let's go back to December, 1, 1955. Let's go south to Montgomery, Alabama. Let's listen to a conversation between a white bus driver and a black woman named Rosa Parks. She is sitting down in the front of the bus.

Bus Driver: *(irritated)* OK, lady, move to the back of the bus! Move to the back of the bus!

(Rosa Parks says nothing and stays in her seat)

Bus Driver: Lady, I told you to move to the back of the bus! You know, that's the law!

(Rosa Parks, silent and looking out the window.)

Bus Driver: *(gets up, goes to her seat, very angry)* I told you to go to the back of the bus. Now, get going! The front seats are for Whites only. You know that. See that man. He wants your seat!

Passenger: Yeah, lady. You don't belong here. Your place is in the back of the bus.

Rosa Parks: I'm sitting right here. I'm tired, and I'm not moving.

Chorus: Rosa, Rosa,
Do not move.
You have a right
To sit where you are.
You have a right
To sit where you are.
Don't move, Rosa,
Don't you move!

Bus Driver: Lady, don't make trouble! You don't want me to call the cops, do you?

Rosa Parks: Do what you want. I'm sitting right here. I'm not moving, and that's that!

(Bus Driver calls a policeman and brings him on to the bus.)

Bus driver: *(to policeman)* Hey, officer! This lady won't sit at the back of the bus. She knows it's the law. We all know that's the law, Whites in front, Negroes in back!

Martin Luther King, Jr.'s Birthday • 77

Policeman: Look, lady, don't make any trouble. Just go and sit at the back of the bus, and everything will be all right.

Rosa Parks: I have a right to sit right here. It's my right to sit here. I'm not moving.

Policeman: Lady, if you don't go to the back of the bus, I'll have to take you to jail. Is that what you want—jail? So don't make trouble; just get up and move.

Chorus: Don't move,
Rosa Parks.
Stay where you are.
Sit where you are.
You have a right
To sit where you are.

Rosa Parks: I'm not going to the back of the bus. I'm sitting right here. This is my seat!

Policeman: OK, if that's the way you want it! *(Policeman handcuffs her and takes her off the bus to jail.)*

Narrator: Soon, the Black community heard about this. It was shocked. First, they raised money to get her out of jail. Then they met with Martin Luther King, Jr., their leader, to decide what to do. They were ready to take action.

Dr. King: They took Rosa to jail? Incredible! Now is the time to act. It's time to stand up against this terrible discrimination. It's time to protest!

Supporter: But what can we do? We need a plan so that the white community will listen to us, so that laws will be changed. What can we do?

Dr. King: The business community understands only one thing — money. Money talks! We will refuse to ride their buses. We'll get them where it hurts — in their pocketbooks.

Supporter: What do you mean?

Dr. King: We will boycott the buses. We will stop all transportation by bus. We will not take buses until this discrimination ends! Their buses will be empty, and they will lose money!

Supporter: But how will we get to our jobs?

Chorus: Ride your bikes
Go on foot!
And car pool, too!
Ride your bikes
Go on foot!
And car pool, too!
Don't ride the bus!
Go on foot.

Dr. King: And remember, no violence, no fighting. If they take us to jail, they take us to jail! We will protest quietly, non-violently, like Mahatma Gandhi did. It won't be easy, but we are ready!

Chorus: For eight long months
The people walked.
They car pooled, too.
They rode their bikes.
They rode no buses
For eight long months,
For eight long months!

Narrator: Because of that, buses were running empty, and the city was losing thousands and thousands of dollars.

Bus Official: We must do something. Our buses are empty, and we are going bankrupt. This can't continue! We can't continue like this.

Narrator: Finally, the city and Martin Luther King, Jr.'s group came to an agreement. Black people were allowed to sit where they wanted. It was a victory, and it was justice.

Chorus: It was a victory
And justice too!
To sit on the bus
Where you wanted to!

Rosa Parks: That was really some day — the day I wouldn't go to the back of the bus! I was scared, but I wasn't going to move for anybody. And I know it was the right thing to do. Yes, it was the right thing to do.

Narrator: But the fight was not over. There was still segregation in such places as hotels and restaurants. There were many more protests.

Martin Luther King, Jr.'s Birthday • 79

Dr. King: That's right. In 1963, we had a huge march on Washington. We marched for justice. We marched for equality. Over 200,000 people came. It was wonderful! I spoke, and the nation listened.

Narrator: In 1964, Congress passed the Civil Rights Act. It was the strongest civil rights bill in American history, and it legally ended segregation. It was a real victory for black people everywhere and for America, too.

Valentine's Day

Valentine's Day is always on February 14. It is not a national holiday. It

is a day when people exchange messages of love and caring. They send cards

to each other. They buy flowers and chocolates to give to their loved ones.

In schools, children often make their own Valentine's cards.

Prepare for the play. Listen and write.

There are _____

_____

_____

_____

_____

_____

_____

Background Reading for the Play

Pocahontas was an Indian Princess, the daughter of Powhatan, Chief of the Algonquin Tribe. She was a beautiful, lively young girl when she first met John Smith, an English explorer. He and his group had settled nearby at Jamestown, the first English colony in America. The year was 1607.

When the English came, there was conflict between the English and the Indians. One day John Smith was captured. The Indians were going to kill him. Pocahontas saw this. She begged her father, Powhatan, not to kill him, and lay her own head on the spot meant for his head. Her father let him go, and John Smith was saved.

Pocahontas often visited Jamestown bringing food and furs to the colony. She was an important link between the two cultures. Unfortunately, John Smith returned to England, and soon there was war. Pocahontas was kidnapped and taken to live on a ship. Finally, when she was released, she chose to live among the English and became a Christian. Shortly after, she met John Rolfe. They fell in love and married. Peace was restored once again between the English and the Indians.

A year later, along with their new-born son, they took a trip to England. When John and Pocahontas were ready to return to America, Pocahontas became very ill. And within days, she died. She was only twenty-two. All were shocked by the death of this beautiful Indian Princess who had helped others so much.

Answer

1. Pocahontas was an Indian _____.

2. John Smith was an English _____.

3. One day John Smith was _____.

4. Pocahontas _____ John Smith.

5. Pocahontas often _____ the Jamestown Colony.

6. She was _____ and taken to live on a ship.

7. After she was released, she _____ in love with John Rolfe.

8. They took their new-born _____ to England

9. When they were ready to return to America, Pocahontas became very _____.

10. She was only twenty-two when she _____.

Pronounce

capture	colony	explore	expedition
message	accident		Pocahontas
injure	prisoner		
homesick		establish	
Jamestown			

they've captured him	they've killed many of us
they've taken our land	you've saved my life
I haven't seen him	the men you've captured
you've no right	what've you brought
he'd been injured	he'd returned

Match

1. _____ An explorer   A. contains information.

2. _____ The English   B. is to catch someone or some animal.

3. _____ A colony   C. is a place that belongs to another country.

4. _____ An expedition   D. travels in unknown lands.

5. _____ To capture   E. is a captured person.

6. _____ A message   F. is to miss one's own country.

7. _____ An accident   G. established a colony in Jamestown.

8. _____ To injure   H. is a long journey.

9. _____ To be homesick   I. is an unexpected problem.

10. _____ A prisoner   J. is to hurt.

Copy and say

1. *An explorer* _____

2. _____

3. _____

4. _____

5. _____

6. _____

7. _____

8. _____

9. _____

10. _____

FOR LOVE, OUR NEXT ATTRACTION

Pocahontas

The incredible story of a young Indian Princess

She stood up for peace. She stood up for love.
But fate was cruel.

Talk about the poster.

The ESL Playhouse

PRESENTS

Pocahontas

The incredible story of a young Indian Princess

PRODUCED BY   _____

DIRECTED BY   _____

THE CAST

Narrator   _____

John Smith   _____

Powhatan   _____

Pocahontas   _____

Indian 1   _____

Indian 2   _____

Settler 1   _____

Settler 2   _____

John Rolfe   _____

Chorus   _____

_____

_____

_____

TIME: 1607

PLACE: Jamestown, Virginia

STORY: Pocahontas plays an important part in keeping peace between the White settlers and the Indians.

Your Playbill

Pocahontas

Narrator: John Smith was an explorer who came to the New World. In 1607, he established the first English colony in Jamestown, Virginia. One day while on an expedition, John Smith was captured by the Indians.

Indian 1: Come with us John Smith! You and your settlers don't belong here. We shall take you to our chief. You shall die!

John Smith: *(struggling)* I do no harm. Let me go! Let me go!

Indian 2: No! This is not your land, not yours! We will take you to Chief Powhatan. He will decide what to do with you. Come!

Chorus: A little girl, twelve years old,
Was watching this.
Pocahontas was watching this.
Pocahontas was watching this.

Pocahontas: Oh, no! They've captured John Smith! I must help him. I must run to my father. He must help John Smith. Father! Father!

Powhatan: Yes, my daughter. You are out of breath. Have you been running and playing?

Pocahontas: Father, father! They've captured John Smith! They've captured him!

Powhatan: Then, daughter, he must die. These white men have killed many of us. They've taken our land. Now he must die!

Pocahontas: Oh! no, father! Spare him! Spare him! He must not die.

Chorus: Spare him! Spare him!
Powhatan, Powhatan
Spare him! Spare him!

Pocahontas: Please, father! I beg you! Let him go! He is my friend!

Powhatan: *(Raises his hand)* Stop! Do not kill him. This man shall go free. Set him free.

John Smith: Thank you, Pocahontas, you've saved my life. Thank you, Powhatan. From now on our people shall live in peace.

Chorus: She saved his life.
She saved his life.
Pocahontas saved his life!

Pocahontas: Now, go in peace. Go in peace.

Narrator: For the next few years there was peace. Pocahontas often visited Jamestown, bringing messages from her father and food and fur for clothing.

John Smith: Hello, Pocahontas! Good to see you, my little friend! What have you for us today?

Pocahontas: My father sends you corn that you may have enough for the winter and some furs that you may be warm.

John Smith: Thank you, Pocahontas. You are a good friend. I have something for your father, also. Here are beads for him.

Narrator: And so it continued for a few years. There was peace between the English people and the Indians. But then one day when Pocahontas came, John Smith was not there.

Pocahontas: Where's my friend, John Smith? I don't see him. Where is he?

Settler 1: John Smith is not here, Pocahontas. He's dead.

Pocahontas: Oh, no. My dear friend, dead? Oh, no! What happened? What happened?

Settler 1: I don't know. I haven't seen him. I heard he had a terrible accident with his gun.

Pocahontas: How very, very sad. I shall miss him!

Narrator: John Smith had, in fact, been injured by a gunshot, but he wasn't dead. He'd returned to England to take care of his injury. Soon, with John Smith gone, the Indians and the settlers began fighting again, and something terrible happened. Pocahantas was kidnapped.

Settler 2: Come with us, Pocahontas, you are our prisoner. Come with us!

Pocahontas: Oh, no! No! No! I am your friend!

Chorus: They took Pocahontas
And put her on a boat.
They took Pocahontas
And put her on a boat.

Powhatan: Release my daughter. Release my daughter! You have no right to keep my daughter.

Settler 2: We shall release her when you release the men you've captured.

Narrator: Ten months passed, and then Pocahontas was freed. But she didn't return to her village. She settled near the English in Jamestown. There she became a Christian. One day, she met a young man.

John Rolfe: Pocahontas, I am John Rolfe. I have seen you many times, and I have heard that you have done much to build friendship between the settlers here and your nation. You are a very interesting person, *(aside)* and beautiful, too.

Pocahontas: Thank you, Mr. Rolfe. You are very kind.

Narrator: Pocahontas and John became friends, and their friendship became love. Rolfe finally proposed marriage to Pocahontas.

John Rolfe: I love you, Pocahontas! I shall ask your father for your hand in marriage. It will be good for both of our nations, this marriage.

Pocahontas: Yes, John, I love you also, and I shall be your wife.

Narrator: So on April 5, 1614, John Rolfe and Pocahontas, who was now called Rebecca, got married. The marriage brought peace and good will once again. And then, one year later:

John Rolfe: Pocahontas, let us go to London to visit my family. They want to meet you and our little son. The Royal Family wants to meet you, too. Pocahontas you are famous!

Narrator: Pocahontas was famous. Everyone wanted to meet this beautiful Indian Princess. She even met John Smith again! He was now living in London. But, it was not the same as in their happy days in Jamestown.

Pocahontas: *(to her husband)* Oh, John, I am homesick. I want to return to America. I want to return to our home. When can we leave, John? When?

John Rolfe: Soon, my dear, very soon.

Narrator: However, when they were all ready to sail, Pocahontas became very ill. She didn't get better. She became weaker and weaker. Finally, she was taken off the boat, too weak to make the journey.

Pocahontas: John, I am too ill. I shall not get well. I shall die. John, do not be sad. All must die. It is enough that our son lives. Do not be sad, John.

John Rolfe: No, no! Don't leave me, Pocahontas! I love you! Don't leave me!

Narrator: Pocahontas died soon after. She was twenty-two years old.

Chorus: Pocahontas, Pocahontas
We will always
Remember you.
We will always
Remember you.

Narrator: Yes, Pocahontas, we will always remember you.

Presidents' Day

Two of America's greatest presidents, Washington and Lincoln, were born in February. First, Washington's birthday on February 22 was a national holiday. Then Congress made a national holiday for Lincoln, born on February 12. But two holidays just days apart was not a good idea, so we now have Presidents' Day, a holiday that honors both of them on the third Monday in February.

Prepare for the play. Listen and write.

Both Washington and Lincoln
_____

_____

_____

_____

_____

_____

_____

Background Reading for the Play

After the colonies declared their independence, war began with the British. The colonies needed a leader for their small Colonial Army. There was none better than General George Washington. He was a strong leader who was loved by all, especially his men.

Still there were huge problems. The Colonial Army was not strong. It was not like the professional army of the British who had warm clothes, good equipment, and most of all, experience.

At the beginning, all they could do was retreat or run away from the British. The Colonial Army needed a victory very badly. Washington's army and the people at home were getting discouraged.

Finally an opportunity came. Washington decided to attack on Christmas night. He knew the British army was camped across the Delaware River in a place called Trenton, New Jersey. He knew that this army was made up of Hessian soldiers from Germany, and they would be celebrating Christmas, singing, drinking, and playing cards. No one, they thought, would attack on a bitter cold night like this.

No one except Washington! He crossed the icy Delaware River with his small army and easily captured 900 sleeping Hessians. It was a great victory for the Colonial Army and for the colonists. It was the turning point of the war, and Washington was a hero.

Answer

1. The colonies needed a _____ for their army.

2. Washington was a _____ leader.

3. The _____ army was not strong.

4. They needed a _____.

5. Washington decided to attack on _____ night.

6. The _____ army was in Trenton.

7. The Hessians were soldiers from _____.

8. The colonial army crossed the icy Delaware _____.

9. They _____ 900 Hessians.

10. It was a great _____ for the Colonial Army.

Pronounce

frozen	surprise	Hessians	discouraged
	expect	Trenton	New Jersey
patriot	defeat	Princeton	
victory	morale		Massachusetts
dangerous	prepared	Delaware	

we'll win	we'll follow you	it'll be a surprise
we'll attack	they'll be drinking	they'll see us
we'll strike at night	they'll take us across	it'll be too late

Match

1. _____ To be discouraged   A. it can hurt you.

2. _____ Morale   B. is ice.

3. _____ Victory   C. is the opposite of defeat.

4. _____ A surprise   D. is to lose.

5. _____ To expect   E. means to lose hope.

6. _____ To be prepared   F. love their country.

7. _____ Frozen water   G. is the spirit of a person or people.

8. _____ If something is dangerous   H. is to believe something will happen.

9. _____ To be defeated   I. is an unexpected event.

10. _____ Patriots   J. is to be ready.

Copy and say

1. *To be discouraged* _____

2. _____

3. _____

4. _____

5. _____

6. _____

7. _____

8. _____

9. _____

10. _____

The Victory that saved the Revolution

Washington

Crosses the Delaware

With one bold stroke, the general risks everything.
Disaster or Victory? Disgrace or Glory?
This night decides the fate of the nation.

Talk about the poster.

The ESL Playhouse

Proudly Presents

Washington Crosses the Delaware

PRODUCED BY   _____

DIRECTED BY   _____

THE CAST

Narrator	_____
General George Washington	_____
Officer	_____
Hessian Soldier 1	_____
Hessian Soldier 2	_____
Colonial Soldier	_____
Colonist 1	_____
Colonist 2	_____
Chorus	_____
	_____
	_____
	_____

TIME: Christmas night, 1776

PLACE: The Delaware River

STORY: Washington makes a surprise attack on the British army.

Your Playbill

Washington Crosses the Delaware

Narrator: When the American colonies decided to separate from Great Britain, George Washington was asked to be the leader of the army. It was not a strong army. The men were not experienced. They didn't have warm clothes or shoes, and there was little to eat. They lost battle after battle.

Chorus: No clothes, no shoes!
No warm clothes or heavy shoes!
How can we fight a war like that?
How can we fight a war like that?

Officer: General Washington, we are tired, cold, and hungry. We want to go home. We are discouraged. We haven't won a battle yet.

Chorus: Morale was low,
Very, very low,
Because they had won
No battles at all.
None at all!

Washington: Be strong, men! We'll win yet! Be strong!

Officer: General Washington, we believe in you. We'll follow wherever you go. But General Washington, we need a victory. The people at home need a victory, too.

Washington: I have a plan. It'll be a surprise attack on the enemy. They will not expect it. We have a good chance of victory, but we must keep it secret.

Officer: What is it, General? What is it?

Washington: We'll attack Christmas night. They will not expect us. They'll all be drinking and celebrating Christmas. They will not be prepared.

Officer: But General, they're across the Delaware, camped on the other side of the river. They'll see us coming!

Washington: We'll strike at night, when it's dark. Our boats will come in the dead of night when they're sleeping.

Officer: The river is frozen in places, General. How will we get across? The wind is strong, and the weather is terrible. Rowing will be very difficult!

Washington: We have strong oarsmen who can help us. They are experienced sailors and fishermen from Massachusetts. They'll take us across. This is our only chance. If we wait longer, it'll be too late.

Chorus: They got in boats
In the dead of the night.
On Christmas night
They crossed the river
The icy, icy Delaware.

Hessian Soldier 1: Look! I think I see something in the distance.

Hessian Soldier 2: Ah, it's nothing. It's the fog. It's only the fog. Here, have another drink.

Soldier 1: Sure, I'll have another. Keeps me warm on this cold, cold night.

Soldier 2: Let's go inside where it's warm. Nothing's happening out here.

Soldier 1: No, nothing at all. Say, did you give that note to our commander?

Soldier 2: Yes, but he just put in his pocket to read later. He was too busy to read it. He was busy playing cards.

Chorus: That note, that note!
Was a very important note.
It came from a spy,
An American spy
To warn the British
That Washington
Was about to attack.
But nobody read it.
Nobody read it!

Narrator: The trip across the Delaware was cold and dangerous. Large chunks of ice were everywhere. But very slowly and very quietly, Washington and his men made it to the other side. The enemy was sleeping, too drunk to fight.

Officer: Look, they're sleeping. Quickly, get their guns! *(The soldiers collect the guns.)*

Hessian Soldier 1: *(waking up)* What - what's happening? Who are you?

Colonial Soldier: Surprise! My good German friends. You are our prisoners! We are the colonial army.

Chorus: The first big victory,
The first big victory,
Washington's men
Had their first big victory!
Hooray for Washington!
And the Colonials, too!

Washington: Men, let's move on! Let's not wait. Our next attack is on Princeton. The British are camped there. We will surprise them, too!

Colonial Soldier: We are ready, General. We are ready!

Narrator: They marched into Princeton and defeated the British army there as well.

Colonist 1: Have you heard the great news? General Washington and our army have had two victories!

Colonist 2: Isn't that wonderful! Our little army is defeating the great British army. Why, it's amazing!

Colonist 1: Maybe we can win this war, after all.

Colonist 2: Of course, we can! We can win, and we will! But, now we must all support General Washington and his army. We are patriots!

Narrator: The mood in the colonies began to change. Victory was possible. The discouraged colonists began to support the war. They proudly called themselves patriots.

Chorus: Patriots!
We are patriots!
Let us support
Our brave army
And General Washington, too!

Washington: Gentlemen, this war isn't over yet. We have a long way to go, but you have proven yourselves to be good, strong soldiers. Yes, you are good, strong soldiers! I am proud of you, men!

Colonial Soldier: General, many of us who were planning to go home are going to stay with you. We will fight with you to the end.

Narrator: And they did just that. Finally, in 1781, the long war was over. When it was time to elect a new president, a first president for the new nation, there was no question who that would be. It would be George Washington. For the new American nation, Washington was always "First in war, first in peace, and first in the hearts of his countrymen."

Chorus: Washington! Washington!
First in war
First in peace
First in the hearts of his countrymen!

Saint Patrick's Day

Saint Patrick's Day is celebrated on March 17. It is not a national holiday, but it is

a very important day for Irish-Americans. In some U.S. cities there are big parades.

Everybody wears green clothes. The green shamrock leaf, which is a symbol for

Ireland, can be seen everywhere.

Prepare for the play. Listen and write.

Irish immigrants

_____

_____

_____

_____

_____

_____

_____

Background Reading for the Play

One of the most influential families in American politics is the Kennedy family. John F. Kennedy, 35th president of the U.S., was the great-grandson of Patrick Kennedy, who came to America from Ireland in 1840. Patrick was a penniless farmer, who settled in Boston, Massachusetts, where many Irish had settled.

John F. Kennedy's father, Joseph, was a self-made millionaire. He and his wife, Rose, had nine children. The parents raised their children in a close, but strict, Catholic family. They taught the children loyalty and duty to the family. Family always came first in everything they did. And all were expected to excel.

The family spent its summers on Cape Cod in a huge summer home where the children swam, sailed, and lived a privileged life. Politics was often the main topic at the dinner table.

When John ran for President, the whole family campaigned actively: mother, father, brothers, sisters, even in-laws. It was a family effort, and John won. The country was fascinated with the young couple and their two small children who occupied the White House. Tragically, John was assassinated while in office. It was a huge loss for the nation.

Answer

1. John F. Kennedy was the _____ of an Irish immigrant.

2. Patrick Kennedy settled in _____, _____.

3. John's father was a self-made _____.

4. He and his wife had _____ children.

5. The children were expected to _____.

6. They spent their summers in a huge home on _____ _____.

7. The main topic at the dinner table was _____.

8. When John ran for president the whole _____ campaigned for him.

9. The Kennedys occupied the White House with their two _____.

10. John was _____ while in office.

Pronounce

tragic	support	debate	volunteer	jubilation
challenge	campaign	assure	represent	
vision	express			

would you pass the potatoes	I would make sure
I'd like to go	that's what I'd do
you should call her	I couldn't have done it
it would be my pleasure	this would be a good time

Match

1. _____ A depression   A. means to make certain.

2. _____ A tragic event   B. is to say one's thoughts.

3. _____ Politicians   C. argue with each other.

4. _____ A difficult situation D. is great joy and happiness.

5. _____ To express something E. is one's idea for the future.

6. _____ In a debate, two people F. works without pay.

7. _____ Vision   G. occurs when the economy is weak.

8. _____ To assure   H. try to get votes in a political campaign.

9. _____ A volunteer   I. is very sad.

10. _____ Jubilation   J. is a challenge.

Copy and say

A depression
1. _____

2. _____

3. _____

4. _____

5. _____

6. _____

7. _____

8. _____

9. _____

10. _____

The ESL Playhouse

The Kennedys:
An Immigrant Success Story

"In America, anyone can be president,
even if they're Irish!"
With these words, Joe Kennedy challenged his family.
"You'll all have to work together as a family
if you want a Kennedy for President."

Talk about the poster.

The ESL Playhouse
Proudly Presents

The Kennedys:
An Immigrant Success Story

PRODUCED BY   _____

DIRECTED BY   _____

THE CAST

Narrator   _____

John F. Kennedy (Jack)   _____

Joseph Kennedy, his father   _____

Rose Kennedy, his mother   _____

Robert Kennedy, his brother   _____

Joe Kennedy, Jr., his brother   _____

Patricia Kennedy Lawford, his
sister, actor Peter Lawford's wife   _____

Jacqueline Kennedy, John's wife   _____

Chorus   _____

_____

_____

_____

TIME: 1934, 1961

PLACE: The Hyannisport home of the Kennedys on Cape Cod;
The White House

STORY: The Irish American Kennedy family helps John become
President and begin his term in the White House.

Your Playbill

The Kennedys:
An Immigrant Success Story

Narrator: It's dinner time at the Kennedy home. The children are busy eating, talking. They have just said grace. Now Joe, Jr., speaks rudely to John, his younger brother, whom everyone calls Jack.

Joe, Jr: Jack, pass the potatoes! You can't have them all!

Mother: Hush, now Joe! Where are your manners! Ask nicely, and you will get them.

Joe, Jr: Jack, would you *PLEASE* pass the potatoes.

John: Here you are, SIR.

Father: So, children, what did you read in the newspaper today?

John: I read something about the economic depression. Dad, what do you think of President Roosevelt's policies? Do you think he's doing a good job?

Father: It looks that way, Jack. But a lot of people are out of work. In this Depression, many people have no jobs, and there are no jobs for them.

Joe Jr: If I were president, I'd make sure everyone had a job. That's what I'd do!

Father: Joe, someday, you will be president. Why not? In America, anyone can be president, if they set their mind to it, even if they're Irish.

Chorus: A Kennedy for president!
A Kennedy for president!
That's what the family wanted.
A Kennedy for president!

Narrator: Joe, Jr., never became President. Sadly, he was killed in World War II, the first of many personal tragedies for the Kennedy family. John, however, was lucky; he came back as a hero. Then he went into politics. He became a U.S. Representative; then a U.S. Senator. Finally, in 1960, with his father's urging, he ran for President.

Mother: All of us will help, Jack. You will need all of us to get elected. We'll go on TV. I'll meet with women's groups. Girls, you can do that, too. We'll make phone calls. We'll make speeches. We'll do whatever we can. And we won't stop!

Patricia: Peter and I have a lot of friends in Hollywood. Most movie stars love you, Jack. I know they'll support you. I'll start campaigning right away!

Jackie: And, Jack, I can travel with you, even take the children! It'll be good for the public to see a young family man.

Robert: We have a huge job ahead of us. People are not used to having a Catholic in the White House. It's a huge challenge. So, Jack, I'll be your campaign manager. We'll get you in the White House, you'll see.

Chorus: The family united
As never before.
They gave parties.
They gave teas.
They traveled.
And spoke to everyone.
Vote for John Kennedy!
Vote for John Kennedy!
For President!

Robert: Jack, perhaps you should call Mrs. Martin Luther King, Jr. Her husband is in jail. He needs help. I think we should help to get him out of jail. We need to support Civil Rights in America.

John: Of course! That's the right thing to do. I'll call now.

Narrator: And that's what he did. He spoke with Mrs. King, expressing his support for Civil Rights. And then he and his opponent, Richard Nixon, held a debate on TV.

Jackie: Jack, when you go on TV for the debates with Nixon, be sure to look good. Be rested, look strong. It's so important. Millions will be watching you.

John: Good advice, Jackie. Thanks. I like TV, but I know that television can make you or break you.

Chorus: John looked good.
Very, very good.
He was tan.
He looked strong.
Nixon looked bad.
Very, very bad.
He looked sick.

Narrator: Jack won the debate. He looked better and spoke better than Nixon. It was an important TV victory. It was a close election, but John F. Kennedy became president, the first Catholic and youngest man ever to be elected president.

Mother: We did it! We did it! Jack, you are President!

John: I couldn't have done it without my family. Every one of you worked so hard. Thank you, thank you. Robert, I still need your help. I want you to be my Attorney General.

Robert: It would be my pleasure, Mr. President!

John: Now, I want to start thinking about the Inaugural Address. It's an important speech. America is looking for a new direction. I must capture the true vision and spirit of America.

Narrator: And he did just that. Here is part of what he said:

John: And so my fellow Americans, ask not what your country can do for you. Ask what you can do for your country!

Chorus: And so my fellow Americans
Ask not what your country
Can do for you!
Ask what you can do
For your country!

Jackie: That was a wonderful speech, Jack. I'm so proud of you!

John: And I'm proud of you, too, Jackie. The nation loves you. You helped me become President. Now, there's work to be done.

Robert: So, Mr. President, what's the first order of business?

John: I want to establish a Peace Corps and have volunteers go to different countries to teach and give technical support. This will be good for America. It will be good for other countries, too. It's a good way to establish friendship among nations.

Narrator: So, a Peace Corps was established. Young people volunteered to serve their country.

Chorus: The Peace Corps,
The Peace Corps,
Young people volunteered
To teach English,
To work on farms,
To give support,
In all corners of the world.

Narrator: It was a very successful program. And then John traveled to Europe.

Jackie: Good luck, Jack. I hope your trip to Europe is successful.

John: Thanks. Jackie. This would also be a good time to visit Ireland.
I would like to go to the village where my great-grand-father lived.
I think it's important to go back to your roots.

Narrator: The Irish welcomed him with jubilation. They said their son had come home.

Memorial Day

Memorial Day began as a day to remember the soldiers who died during the American Civil War. Nowadays, it is a day to remember all the soldiers who died for their country. People also honor their dead ancestors, and many go to cemeteries to place flowers on the graves of those who have died.

Prepare for the play. Listen and write.

Arlington
_____

_____

_____

_____

_____

_____

_____

_____

Background Reading for the Play

Memorial Day is a national holiday which is celebrated on the fourth Monday in May. It honors the men and women who died serving their country.

A special ceremony is held at Arlington National Cemetery. This cemetery is in Virginia across the Potomac River from Washington, D.C. On Memorial Day, the President visits Arlington National Cemetery in order to pay tribute to those who died for their country. He lays a wreath at the Tomb of the Unknowns.

The Tomb has the remains of four soldiers whose names are unknown. It is a very special site and is guarded by an honor guard that marches at the Tomb twenty-four hours a day, every day, three-hundred sixty-five days a year. The changing of the guard is especially interesting to see.

Thousands of tourists visit Arlington National Cemetery every year. They also visit the John F. Kennedy Memorial where an eternal flame burns.

Many Americans celebrate Memorial Day at home by visiting a cemetery, watching parades, and having picnics with family and friends.

Answer

1. Memorial Day is on the _____ Monday in May.

2. It honors the men and women who died _____ their country.

3. The Cemetery is across the _____ from Washington, D.C.

4. The _____visits Arlington National Cemetery on Memorial Day.

5. The President lays a wreath at the _____ of the Unknowns.

6. The Tomb is _____ by an honor guard.

7. The _____ of the guard is interesting to see.

8. The _____ flame on the Kennedy Memorial burns all night and day.

9. Thousands of _____ visit Arlington National Cemetery.

10. Many Americans visit a _____ and have picnics on Memorial Day.

Pronounce

vigil	decorate	ceremony	conclude	eternal
silence	gratitude	cemetery	deceased	
mansion		military	parade	

We're across the Potomac	It's a very special time
that's where they're buried	that's right
there's one soldier	he's called an honor guard
it's a beautiful ceremony	yes, that's true
it's wonderful	there's lots to see
it's a tradition	

Match

1. _____ Dead people   A. means to end something.

2. _____ A vigil   B. is thankfulness.

3. _____ Silence   C. is a very large, beautiful home.

4. _____ A ceremony   D. are buried in a cemetery.

5. _____ To decorate   E. is a line of people marching.

6. _____ Gratitude   F. is to arrange in a pleasing way.

7. _____ To conclude   G. refers to a dead person.

8. _____ An eternal flame   H. is the opposite of noise.

9. _____ A parade   I. is a planned event, like a funeral.

10. _____ The deceased   J. burns forever.

11. _____ A mansion   K. is a constant watch.

Copy and say

1. *Dead people* _____

2. _____

3. _____

4. _____

5. _____

6. _____

7. _____

8. _____

9. _____

10. _____

11. _____

DON'T FORGET OUR MEMORIAL DAY SPECIAL PRODUCTION

The Heroes at Arlington

Who passes here with solemn tread, with solemn tread?
Who pauses here to honor the dead, to honor the dead?
Here lie heroes who died unknown, all unknown,
Except to God, and to God alone.

Talk about the poster.

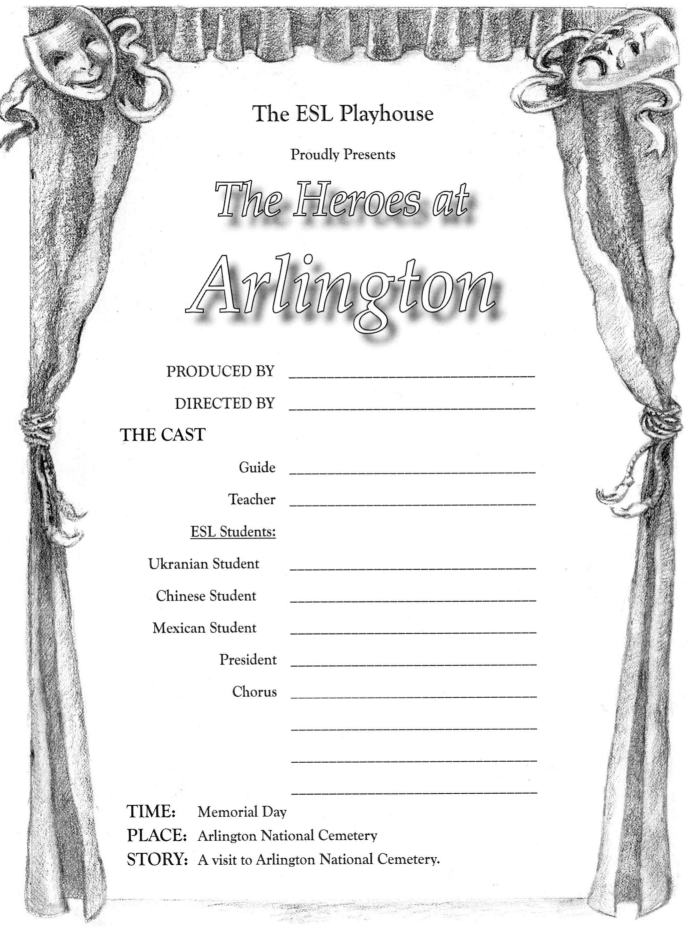

The ESL Playhouse

Proudly Presents

The Heroes at Arlington

PRODUCED BY _____

DIRECTED BY _____

THE CAST

Guide _____

Teacher _____

<u>ESL Students:</u>

Ukranian Student _____

Chinese Student _____

Mexican Student _____

President _____

Chorus _____

_____

_____

_____

TIME: Memorial Day

PLACE: Arlington National Cemetery

STORY: A visit to Arlington National Cemetery.

Your Playbill

The Heroes at Arlington

Guide: Welcome to Arlington National Cemetery in Virginia. We're across the Potomac River and can see Washington, D.C. As you know, this is the largest national cemetery in the U.S. We have thousands of visitors every day, but Memorial Day is a very special time to visit.

Chorus: On Memorial Day,
On Memorial Day,
We honor the men
And the women
Who fought and died.
We honor them all
On Memorial Day!

Guide: Today, we have special ceremonies for those who died for our country. The President will be here. He'll lay a wreath at the Tomb of the Unknowns to honor them. He'll give a speech to the nation.

Chorus: The President will come
And lay a wreath,
A beautiful wreath
At the Tomb.
To honor all,
To honor all
Who fought and died.
Who fought and died!

Ukrainian: We studied about The Tomb of the Unknowns. That's where soldiers who have no names are buried.

Chinese: That's right. Let's go and take a look at it.

Teacher: Students, look at the writing on the Tomb. What does it say?

Chorus: It says :
"Here Rests In Honored Glory
An American Soldier
Known Only to God."

Mexican: Look! There's a soldier marching at the Tomb.

Guide: A soldier marches in front of the tomb twenty-four hours a day, every day, 365 days a year—in any weather. He marches to honor the unknown soldiers. He's called an honor guard.

Chorus: An Honor Guard
Marching in silence
Keeping vigil
At the Tomb.
Marching in silence
Keeping vigil
Day and night
Night and day
All day, all night.

Guide: If you wait a little while, you can see the Changing of the Guard. It's a beautiful ceremony. One soldier leaves and another takes over.

Chinese: We'd like to know more about this place. Look at those flags at each gravesite, thousands of them! Are they here all the time?

Guide: Oh, no, they decorate the graves this way on Memorial Day in May.

Mexican: Is it true that originally Memorial Day celebrated only the soldiers of the Civil War?

Guide: Yes, that's true. At first, this was the cemetery for the soldiers of the Civil War. Shortly after that war, some women came and decorated the graves. It was called Decoration Day. Today Memorial Day is in memory of all who have died in service to their country.

Teacher: Look, I see that the President has arrived. Sh! Let's listen!

(President arrives and lays a wreath at the Tomb of the Unknowns.)

President: My fellow citizens, ladies and gentlemen of the Armed Forces, veterans all. Today we set aside a special day to honor all those who fought and died for our freedom. Today, we remember them all; we honor them all. We give them our deep gratitude. We remember that they gave their lives for us.

Guide: The President will now ask for a moment of silence.

President: Let us remember today our fallen heroes. Let us remember their courage. Let us remember that freedom is not easily won. Let us work for and protect this freedom everywhere. So help us God! Let us have a moment of silence for them.

(silence)

Guide: *(quietly)* The ceremonies will now conclude as a bugler plays "Taps." This is a tune is used in the military for "lights out" at the end of the day.

Chorus: Day is done
Gone the sun
From the lakes
From the hills
From the sky
All is well
Safely rest
God is nigh.

Guide: So, students and friends, that's the way Memorial Day is celebrated in Arlington National Cemetery. It's a very special ceremony. I hope you all enjoyed it.

Teacher: We enjoyed it very much. It's wonderful to be here. Now we want to visit other places while we are here.

Guide: Then you must be sure to see the John F. Kennedy Memorial with its eternal flame.

Ukrainian: We shouldn't miss that. His brother, Robert F. Kennedy, is buried near there, too.

Guide: Also don't miss the home of Robert E. Lee, the famous Civil War general. It's a beautiful mansion. It's on these grounds. There's lots to see at Arlington National Cemetery.

Mexican: Thank you for showing us around. This has been a very special Memorial Day. We'll have much to tell our family and friends when we get back home.

Chinese: What do you think your family and friends are doing today?

Teacher: Like many Americans, they go to a cemetery on Memorial Day. They decorate the graves with flowers.

Chinese: We do that in our country, too. We often even bring food to the cemetery and sweep the gravesite. We have a special day for that.

Ukrainian: In Ukraine, we sometimes bring flowers and food and a drink in memory of the person who passed away. Everybody remembers the deceased in their own special way.

Mexican: In Mexico, we bring food and have a picnic by the graveside. Sometimes, we even bring our guitars and sing, especially if that person loved music. That is our tradition.

Teacher: It is also an American tradition to have a Memorial Day picnic with family and friends, but that is done at home in the backyard.

Guide: Well, friends, it seems that each culture has its own way of remembering those who died. For now, enjoy the rest of your day at Arlington National Cemetery. And, as we say here in the South, Y'all come back!

Chorus: So that's how it is
On Memorial Day.
Veterans and childern
March in parades
In towns and cities
Everywhere.
And families gather
For picnics and fun
And to remember those
Who are not longer here.

Independence Day - The Fourth of July

Independence Day is always celebrated on the Fourth of July. It's a day

of parades, picnics and, of course, fireworks. All across America,

people gather in the evening to await the first explosion that starts the

fireworks display.

Prepare for the play. Listen and write.

The thirteen _____

_____

_____

_____

_____

_____

_____

Background Reading for the Play

In 1776, the relations between the thirteen American colonies and Great Britain reached the breaking point. Delegates from the thirteen colonies gathered in Philadelphia to write a document that would declare independence.

Thomas Jefferson, a young lawyer and patriot, was chosen to write this document. He knew how important his task was, and he wrote a magnificent document. He expressed what was in the hearts and minds of the colonists. They did not want taxation without representation. They did not want soldiers in their towns during peacetime.

On July 2, 1776, the delegates from all thirteen colonies signed the Declaration. It was adopted on July 4. Signing it was not easy. If the signers were caught, they would surely be hanged. Messengers on horseback carried copies of the document to the colonies.

The Declaration of Independence inspired the colonists. They cheered when it was read in towns and villages throughout the colonies. And it inspired General George Washington, the leader of the colonial army, and his soldiers.

Today, the original Declaration of Independence is in a special case at the National Archives Building in Washington, D. C. During the day, a guard stands by to protect it. In the evening, it is lowered into a basement vault so that it cannot be destroyed or stolen. It is one of America's most treasured documents.

Answer

1. In 1776, delegates from the _____ colonies met in Philadelphia.

2. They wanted to _____ independence.

3. Thomas Jefferson was chosen to _____ the document.

4. The colonists did not want _____ without representation.

5. If the signers were caught, they would be _____.

6. Messengers on _____ carried the document to the colonies.

7. The Declaration _____ the colonists.

8. General George Washington was the leader of the _____ army.

9. The original document is in a special case in _____, _____.

10. It is one of America's most _____ documents.

Pronounce

massacre	document	pursuit	independence
tolerate	powerful	adopt	declaration
innocent	messenger		
separate			opportunity

it's time to be free	it's necessary to do so	it's a beautiful document
it's my wish	it was called a massacre	it was my pleasure
it was adopted	it was read	it was cheered

Match

1. _____ To declare

2. _____ In a massacre

3. _____ To tolerate

4. _____ An innocent person

5. _____ To separate from

6. _____ An official paper

7. _____ A powerful message

8. _____ The Almighty

9. _____ To adopt

10. _____ An opportunity

A. is another name for God.

B. is a document.

C. is to state or say something.

D. is to accept and make official

E. many people are killed.

F. is a chance to do something.

G. has not done anything wrong.

H. means to leave.

I. is a very strong statement.

J. is to accept someone or something.

Copy and say

1. To declare _____

2. _____

3. _____

4. _____

5. _____

6. _____

7. _____

8. _____

9. _____

10. _____

THE SMASH HIT OF THE SUMMER

Now at the Playhouse

Fireworks
in Philadelphia

or

We Will All Hang Together

Adams, Franklin, Jefferson, Rush, Lee, Hancock, and Washington – were they traitors or patriots? will the signers hang? Come and see!

Talk about the poster.

The Poster for the Play

The ESL Playhouse

PRESENTS

Fireworks
in Philadelphia

or

We Will All Hang Together

PRODUCED BY   _____

DIRECTED BY   _____

THE CAST

Narrator   _____

<u>The Patriots in Philadelphia:</u>

John Adams   _____

Benjamin Franklin   _____

Thomas Jefferson   _____

Dr. Benjamin Rush   _____

Richard Henry Lee   _____

John Hancock   _____

Messenger   _____

Colonial   _____

George Washington   _____

Soldier   _____

Chorus   _____

_____

_____

_____

TIME: July, 1776

PLACE: State House, Philadelphia, Pennsylvania

STORY: Thomas Jefferson writes the Declaration of Independence, and a nation is born.

Your Playbill

Fireworks in Philadelphia

or

We Will All Hang Together

Narrator: At the beginning of our nation, there were thirteen colonies. They were ruled by King George, III of Great Britain. The colonists were not happy. The King wanted more and more taxes, and his soldiers were everywhere in the colonies.

Chorus: No more taxes!
No more taxes!
They don't want
Any more taxes!

Narrator: But most of all, the colonists didn't like the soldiers in their cities and towns.

Chorus: Take the soldiers
Back to Britain!
Take the soldiers
Back to Britain!
They don't want them
On their streets!

Narrator: Yes, the British soldiers were everywhere. One day, a fight broke out in Boston, and shooting began. Five Americans were killed. It was called a massacre, the Boston Massacre. Colonial leaders began to think about independence.

Adams: Gentlemen, we cannot tolerate what the British are doing! The British have invaded our towns, homes, and countryside. They have killed innocent people! We are not free!

Jefferson: We have written to the King in protest many times, but he hasn't listened to us.

Lee: Now is the time to separate from England! It's time for America to be free and independent! We must tell the King that we will be his colonies no more!

Independence Day • 127

Adams: Yes, that is what we must do, become a free country. Mr. Jefferson, will you write a document of independence?

Jefferson: Yes, of course, I shall be happy to do it. It's necessary to do so.

Narrator: He began writing immediately in that hot spring of '76. "We hold these truths to be self-evident, that all men are created equal."

Chorus: All are equal!
All are equal!
We believe
All men are equal!
And should be free!

Jefferson: Gentlemen, here it is, the Declaration of Independence! It states that we are a free and independent nation, ruled by none.

Franklin: Mr. Jefferson, this is excellent! It's a beautiful and powerful document. No one could have expressed our ideas better than you. It's a beautiful piece of work! Let's sign it.

Jefferson: Thank you, Mr. Franklin. It was my pleasure and my duty.

Rush: Yes, an excellent piece of work. But, you know, if we sign this, the British will hang us.

Chorus: The British will hang you!
The British will hang you!
If they catch you
They will hang you!

Franklin: Dr. Rush, either way, the British will hang us. They do not like our protests and shoot at every opportunity. I say, we must all hang together, or else we shall all hang separately.

Chorus: Sign it! Sign it!
Sign the document
Sign it! Sign it!
Sign the document!

Hancock: Here, let me sign. I shall write in large letters. I want to make sure that the King can read my name without his glasses!

Narrator: So on July 2, 1776, all fifty-six men signed the Declaration of Independence. On July 4, it was adopted.

Rush: And now, to the printer!

Lee: And then by messenger to every colony!

Hancock: I know my friends in Boston will cheer this great day and this great Declaration.

Narrator: The Declaration was indeed cheered wherever the messenger went.

Messenger: Here! Read this! It's great news! Spread the news! Spread the news, now! We are free. We are a free country!

Colonist: A free nation! Finally! This is wonderful, indeed! Let me tell my neighbors!

Chorus: Throughout the land,
It was read.
Throughout the land,
It was cheered!
The Declaration
Was read and cheered!

Narrator: At that time, General George Washington was in New York with his army. War had begun a year earlier, and he was protecting the harbor. He received The Declaration of Independence on July 9.

Washington: Gentlemen, here's our Declaration of Independence! Thank God! This is what we have been waiting for. This is what we are fighting for!

Soldier: Hooray for Liberty and Independence!

Washington: Gentlemen, we have a difficult road ahead of us. We will have many battles. Men, we must all be strong. Be strong! And now, let us show them who we are!

Soldier: General Washington, we are ready to follow you! All of us. We are ready to go wherever you go!

Washington: You are brave men, and we will win this war!

Narrator: And so, after a long, hard struggle, General Washington's army defeated the British. And a new nation was born.

Jefferson: This nation gives each person certain basic rights which are written in the Declaration of Independence.

Chorus: Life, liberty, and
The pursuit of happiness!
Life, liberty, and
The pursuit of happiness!
These are our rights!
These are our rights!
Given to us!

The Dictations

for the exercises, "Prepare for the play. Listen and write."

Labor Day

In the 1800s,   many workers from Europe   came to work   in the factories.

They worked   on the farms.

They built the railroads.

They built the cities.

They worked hard   under difficult conditions   for little money.

They became angry,   and they formed unions   to demand

better working conditions   and more money.

One of the organizers   was Peter McGuire.

Let's read about him.

Columbus Day

Until 1492,   there were not many people   in the Americas.

The people who lived there   are now called "Indians"

or "Native Americans."

The people of Europe   did not know   about these lands   and peoples.

Columbus tried to sail   across the Atlantic Ocean   to reach India

and the East.

But he accidentally discovered   America and its "Indians."

Halloween

People like to tell   ghost stories,   especially at Halloween.

One of America's   first well-known writers   was Washington Irving.

One of his   most famous stories   is "The Legend of Sleepy Hollow."

Our play   is based on   this story.   First, let's read   about the story.

Veterans Day

America has had   many wars,   some big,   some small.

The biggest of all   was World War II.

In Europe   and in Asia   millions of people died.

The German army   controlled Europe.

On June 6, 1944   the allied nations   invaded Europe.

This day is called   D-Day.

It was the beginning   of the end.

The war in Europe   finally ended   on May 8, 1945,   almost one year

after D-Day.

The decision to invade   was not easy.

Thanksgiving

In 1620, a small group of people from England arrived in the New World.

They were called Pilgrims.

The first winter was very difficult.

Many died.

But the community survived.

The Indians helped them grow and find food.

In the fall they celebrated their successful harvest with a feast of thanksgiving to God.

They shared the feast with the Indians.

We will read about their arrival and survival in the New World.

Christmas

Christmas is a time when people try to be generous and give to others.

Christmas carols and stories celebrate love, joy, friendship and charity.

One of the most famous Christmas stories is "A Christmas Carol."

Charles Dickens wrote it in 1843.

It is a story about a man who hated Christmas.

The story is still very popular and is often performed as a play.

New Year's Day

On New Year's Eve,   thousands of people   go to Times Square

   in New York City.

At the top of a building   there is a huge lighted ball.

At one minute   before midnight   the ball begins   to come down.

For the last ten seconds,   everybody counts: "ten, nine, eight,"

Then at 12:00 o'clock   they cheer   and welcome   the new year.

Let's go to Times Square.

Martin Luther King, Jr.'s Birthday

In 1955,   an ordinary black woman   changed history.

In Montgomery, Alabama,   the city buses   were segregated;

Blacks were supposed to   sit in the back   of the bus.

One day,   Rosa Parks   was tired,   and she refused   to move to the back.

Martin Luther King, Jr.   organized a boycott   of the city buses.

Nine years later   the U.S. congress   made segregation illegal.

Valentine's Day

There are   many famous stories   about love and friendship.

In early America,   a young Indian princess,   Pocahontas,

saved the life   of John Smith.

Smith was an English explorer.

Pocahontas became friends   with the English settlers.

Smith returned to England,   but Pocahontas   married John Rolfe,

one of the settlers.

Presidents' Day

Both Washington and Lincoln   were great presidents.

They both served   their country   in difficult times.

Washington was   the first US president,   and he was also

the general who   led the colonies   to victory

in the American Revolution.

This play   is about   one of his famous victories.

Saint Patrick's Day

Irish immigrants started coming to America in large numbers in the Nineteenth century.

They played an important part in the development of the country.

They worked in the factories and they helped build the railroads.

In the cities they became political leaders.

The Kennedy family of Massachusetts reached the highest political office when John F. Kennedy was elected president.

Memorial Day

Arlington National Cemetery is across the river from Washington, D.C.

More than 200,000 soldiers from America's wars are buried there.

It is also the gravesite of John F. Kennedy and other American heroes.

At the cemetery is the Tomb of the Unknown Soldiers — a memorial to the many soldiers who died on the battlefield and were never identified.

Independence Day

The thirteen American colonies   were tired of British rule   and British taxes.

They wanted   their own country.

Several leaders   of the independence movement   gathered in Philadelphia   to write a document   that declared independence   from Great Britain.

Thomas Jefferson   wrote the declaration.

On July 4, 1776,   the Declaration of Independence   was adopted.

Teacher's Notes

First refer to the **student's guide** in the front of this book. This is written for the student, but it will also give you a general idea of how to use the material in this book. As always, use your own best judgement on how to make the best use of the plays and the supporting material. Now here for your consideration are a few suggestions.

The plays can be done in any order, and at any time, although doing a holiday play during the month in which the holiday occurs certainly enhances the vitality of the play. Note that there are no holidays for the months of April, June, and August, and there are two holidays in October, November, January, and February.

Each of the holiday units begins on the first page with an **introduction** to contemporary practices of the holiday. The information here is brief, and you may want to precede the material in the book with a warm-up or additional information about the holiday.

The **dictation** *(Prepare for the play. Listen and write.)* is a bridge between the contemporary observances of the holiday and the play which is associated with the holiday, but which is not necessarily a part of the contemporary scene. By doing this as a dictation as they begin their preparations for doing the play, the students become more activily involved. They listen, write, ask for repetitions, ask for definitions and, quite simply, become more involved with the language and the information. Although, it may be best for you to give the dictation, you can also have a student do it. Note that the sentences in the dictations are broken into phrases for better comprehension. Read the whole sentence first, and then say it phrase by phrase as the students write.

The *Background Reading for the Play* provides more information about the play. It is also, of course, an opportunity to practice reading skills. The accompanying *Answer* section can be used to check comprehension.

The **pronunciation** section *(Pronounce)* features words and phrases that will appear in the play, and which may be new to the students. They may ask for definitions of the words, and it may be good to give them examples and definitions at this time. However, the main point here is to practice the stress patterns. One syllable in each word in English receives the most energy, becoming louder and longer, while the other syllables often collapse, and are spoken quietly and rapidly. This is a very important aspect of English pronunciation, and helping your students acquire the rhythm of spoken English will contribute to a natural-sounding rendition of the play — and their everyday speech. Note that the words are grouped in columns, each column having a similar stress/rhythm pattern.

The phrases give the students the opportunity to practice connected speech. Again, the stress patterns of English are practiced here, and the smooth production of a series of words is the objective. This will give practice in linking and elision. The phrases also exhibit grammatical features such as noun phrases, verb phrases, prepositional phrases and contractions.

The **matching** exercise *(Match)* essentially helps the students understand the meaning and use of the words thay have pronounced and some of the words they will encounter in the play. The words were selected because they were multisyllabic (for pronunciation purposes) and also because they may be unfamiliar words to a low intermediate student.

Having the students *copy* their matches also reinforces the basic sentence pattern of English. The left column of the match is the subject of the sentence and the right column is the predicate. Having them *say* their sentences after they have written them offers another opportunity to work on the stress and rhythm of a complete sentence. By delivering an entire sentence, the students are practicing speaking with natural pauses at the end of phrases, in this case, between the subject and the predicate.

The **illustrated poster** for each play helps the students anticipate the play, and thus, be better prepared to deal with it as they go through the script for the first time. You can also copy the page and post it around the school if the students will be performing it.

The **playbill** can be used as a stimulus for group decision-making. Although you can be the producer and/or the director, you can also have the students choose who will do what and who will take the major speaking parts. Because these plays have a chorus, everybody has a part. As you practice the play, you may want to work with the chorus in one corner of the room, while others practice their lines in another corner. As you work with the chorus, it is important that they speak rhythmically in unison, but at the same time, naturally.

When the play has been thoroughly practiced, you can have them do a dramatic reading with entrances, exits, props, and even sound effects. By videotaping the reading, the students will, naturally, enjoy seeing and hearing themselves, and will also have the opportunity to critique their performance. You can, of course, have them perform the play, making copies of the playbill for the audience.

All but one of these plays are based on U.S. history or folklore and culture - and Americans' love of Dickins' *A Christmas Carol* makes it a part of the culture, too. There is more to teach and discuss about each of these plays than we could put in this book, but each play can serve as a springboard for hours of questioning, research, and important discussion.

Other Publications from Pro Lingua

American Holidays: Exploring Traditions, Customs and Backgrounds. This book of readings is an excellent companion to the plays in this book. Each of the 20 readings in intermediate English also includes several exercises focused on the vocabulary that naturally occurs at each holiday time.

3 More drama- and history-based books by Anne Siebert:

● **All Around America: The Time Traveler's Talk Show.** Students listen to the 18 shows (**2 CDs**) and perform them as a cooperative reading using the book of **show scripts**. The magical host visits high-interest sites around the U.S. answering call-ins by summoning historical figures. The **workbook** gives a pre-reading exercise; then, idiom, comprehension, vocabulary, grammar, writing, and web work.

● **Celebrating American Heroes. The Playbook** is a collection of 13 short plays featuring an interesting group of heroes, from the very famous (Lincoln, Washington, Edison) to the less well-known (Dolley Madison, Jonas Salk, John Muir, Cesar Chavez, Harriet Beecher Stowe). The format of the plays is similar to *Plays for the Holidays* with a few leading characters, a narrator, and a chorus. The **photocopyable Teacher's Guide** includes several pronunciation and vocabulary worksheets. Recordings of the plays are also available on a **cassette** or **CD.**

● **Heroes from American History.** An integrated skills content-based **reader** for intermediate ESL. All the heroes in the playbook (above) are featured as well as Maya Lin, Eleanor Roosevelt, and the "ordinary citizen." There are maps and timelines that bring out the historical context of the times when these heroes lived.

Stranger in Town. This heart warming play in 4 brief acts is about a drifter who attempts to settle down in a small American town. The play is a metaphor for the process of learning and adjusting. The **playbook** can be used for dramatic reading and/or with the **cassette** or CD. This is a powerful listening and acting experience, bringing many personal, cultural, and language insights.

Legends: 52 People Who Made a Difference. 4 biographies of graded difficulty in each of 13 categories. A time line backs each reading relating it to American history. A **double CD** recording is available.

The dramatic art of storytelling is another excellent way to involve your students in speaking effectively and listening critically. The first two of the following books are printed as collections of small cards to be cut from the booklet and used as prompts:

• **Story Cards: North American Indian Tales**. 48 animal stories collected from tribes across North America. The tales explain how the world came to be as it is (How Chipmunk Got its Stripes, etc.) Each story is on a separate card with a colorful illustration by a popular Native American artist.

• **Story Cards: Aesop's Fables**. This collection of beautifully illustrated stories features 48 of Aesop's classic stories, many of them known the world over.

• **The Tales of Nasreddin Hodja** can be used for storytelling or as a reader. Hodja's droll and witty stories are known throughout the world of Islam. A **CD** with all 66 traditional tales is available.

• **Pearls of Wisdom** is a collection of African and Caribbean folktales for listening and reading. The complete package includes the text, an integrated-skills **workbook,** and a recording of the tales by the author, a griot from Benin, that is to be used with the **text** and is available on 2 **CD**s or **cassettes**.